WHEN SHE'S IN THE ROOM

HOW EMPOWERING WOMEN
EMPOWERS THE WORLD

EDWINA DUNN

HarperCollins*Publishers*

HarperCollins*Publishers*
1 London Bridge Street
London SE1 9GF

www.harpercollins.co.uk

HarperCollins*Publishers*
Macken House, 39/40 Mayor Street Upper
Dublin 1, D01 C9W8, Ireland

First published by HarperCollins*Publishers* 2024

1 3 5 7 9 10 8 6 4 2

Text © Edwina Dunn 2024
Foreword © Martha Lane Fox 2024
Persona illustrations by Callum Blake © The Female Lead
Graphs by e-digitaldesign.co.uk

Edwina Dunn asserts the moral right to be identified as the
author of this work

A catalogue record of this book is available from the British Library

HB ISBN 978-0-00-860753-1
PB ISBN 978-0-00-861252-8

Printed and bound in the UK using 100% renewable electricity
at CPI Group (UK) Ltd

This book contains FSC™ certified paper and other controlled
sources to ensure responsible forest management.

For more information visit: www.harpercollins.co.uk/green

To every girl, every woman, who is under-estimated

CONTENTS

CONTENTS

CONTENTS

FOREWORD

by Martha (Lady) Lane Fox, Baroness Lane-Fox of Soho, CBE

I met Edwina in 2014 at the House of Lords. She was exploring a new project called 'What I See' which involved interviewing a wide range of women and filming them answering the question, 'What do you see when you look in the mirror?' The resulting diversity and strength of opinions were fascinating, and I was glad to share my own story. Clearly, this was the beginning of her interest and passion for understanding how women perceive not just their outward appearance, but what they stand for and believe in. Since then, this work and the 1,500 films she created have been shared at the V&A and have become the foundation for The Female Lead, now with nearly 8 million followers.

Not only do Edwina and I share a passion for women's rights, but we share a technology and entrepreneurial background. We both grew up in the years when technology flourished and our businesses became dotcom hits. Mine was Lastminute.com and hers was dunnhumby, which launched Tesco Clubcard. Since selling our businesses, we have both become involved with the internet and social media in different ways. I joined the Board of Twitter and Edwina started to analyse what people love, even more than brands, on social media. In this era of purpose above product, the knowledge of what motivates us as humans and drives us to engage with and feel fulfilled in our lives is something that I know we both care about and feel that we can study and help to implement, as a science and as a platform for good, helping those who can't access technology and are in danger of falling behind.

My work has focused on how technology will affect us all, now and into the future. We are living in an era where technology no longer restricts what we can do but ethical behaviours are now essential to govern the boundaries of right and wrong. People continue to worry about privacy, but eventually regulation will emerge and offer greater safety and protections. That is part of my focus and work in the House of Lords. Excitingly, big data (which Edwina focused on early in her career) will now help us resolve societal issues including cancer and chronic diseases. I believe that there is a golden age coming as we invest in technology, space and the acceleration of learning, with AI helping us to adapt and learn.

I studied Ancient History and am reminded, as I look at Edwina's new book, of the tribe of women in the Mongolian Steppe who were great hunters. Herodotus wrote about this many centuries ago. We now need a new generation of women warriors in technology and many other spheres of influence.

In my experience, when life is precarious, when challenges are great, we forget the differences in sex. We all now need to work together and find better and fairer solutions. Dame Stephanie Shirley started her company in the 1960s. She employed only women as engineers, building software and, radically then, working from home. No one took Stephanie (as she was then) seriously until she signed her name Steve. Then contracts emerged. Her work and impact were incredible. She had 2,000 women working from home on projects including the Polaris submarine and the black box recording device for Concorde.

Women in Parliament are still a minority but the number of women in the tech sector is even smaller. Only 10% of businesses are female-founded. Engineering is only chosen by 4% of women. Just 2% of venture capitalists are female. Technology is changing the world and fast. The most exciting innovation for centuries is now in our hands. And it's such a waste that women are not part of this revolution. We need 1 million new jobs in this sector. And today there are some 800,000 unemployed women. Despite a new generation of great pioneers and advocates such as Anne-Marie Imafidon, Vanessa Sanyauke and Sue Black, the UK needs many more women warriors to empower us digitally and to help fuel our economy.

Half the world is not using the internet. Everyone needs to have a voice and be connected – I fight for a fairer and more responsible internet. We need to make education more accessible and to encourage lifelong learning. Like the great tennis player, Djokovic, it's time to hang a mirror in your bathroom and shout positive things to yourself.

The stories that Edwina collects and shares are important. We all need inspiration and role models. It is truly hard to be what you can't see. Becoming the best version of ourselves requires unwavering determination. You can't become world class without extreme commitment, sacrifice and hard work. We are all working longer, and we are all wanting purpose, not just profit. As Chancellor of the Open University, I see that 71% of its 200,000 students study while in employment, engaging in lifelong learning while in work. I believe that today, you're either busy learning or you're being replaced. The boundaries between work and learning have never been so blurred.

Like me, Edwina is a believer in the Power of Two. She had a great partnership with her partner, Clive Humby. I see it and know it because I have identical twins. So I have a deeply ingrained love of pairs. This Power of Two is all about sharing similar values and vision – a common view of the impact you want to make in the world, shared motivations. Great examples of this in the world of business are Sergey Brin and Larry Page at Google.

I too see a vision of *When She's in the Room*. If we can't get women to the decision-making table, we cannot adequately respond to our need for world-class solutions using data and technology right across our society. Women need to be studied and empowered. We are 50% of the population and not a minority. I believe that this book reveals new evidence around the economic might of women and the logical ways in which we can build a more balanced and inclusive world to the benefit of all.

Martha Lane Fox is a British businesswoman, philanthropist and public servant. She is President of the British Chambers of Commerce and a Crossbench Peer in the UK House of Lords, and sits on multiple boards. She is Chair of WeTransfer and Chancellor of the Open University. She cofounded and chairs Lucky Voice. Martha was UK Digital Champion from 2009 to 2013 and helped create gov.uk. She cofounded lastminute.com in 1998. She is a vocal advocate for human rights, women's rights and social justice.

CHAPTER 1

THE POWER OF TWO: DATA AND STORIES

The Female Lead began on a corner desk with a small team I had hand-picked for the project. Bunched together in this inconspicuous setting, we began to plan. The idea was a simple one. We wanted to help girls access the stories of inspiring women. Storytelling is the oldest wisdom across the world, and today we can bring science and data to our storytelling without losing the magic. Data and stories are rarely blended, but I have always found that they work in perfect unison.

Right from my earliest days of work, I learned that doing everything alone is easier but rarely more effective. If you discover the Power of Two, you create a force that is game-changing. This is a system I created and which centres around partnering with someone with the opposite skill set to yours. You trust in each other's capabilities and direct your focus to where your individual strengths lie.

The Power of Two can be extended to data and stories as they have opposing forces and appeal to different types of people. Data confirms the reality of a situation. It treats all viewpoints as equal, as there is no volume button when it comes to an individual's data input. But 'big data', which is the wisdom of many, provides a comprehensive oversight of a situation – a helicopter view. It has been shown that people working together in groups outperform people working individually in the areas of problem-solving, reasoning and assessment of probability.[1] By using data to aggregate women's voices and differing needs, all that wisdom can be amplified. This is what is so enriching about data insight – you can take all the micro activities and opinions and aggregate them into larger patterns and more prominent robust recommendations. We then arrive at crowdsourced wisdom.

On the other side are stories, which provide the warmth and connection that, as human beings, we need. Statistics might briefly stop us in our tracks, but it is often a fleshed-out story coming from the lips of someone we have grown to admire that is the true rallying cry. Human stories provide the inspiration and offer the momentum for change. They personalise things, providing a connection that data sometimes struggles to establish. Our brains have evolved to interpret and recall stories, not facts and figures. Data has the power to shock, but stories can embrace us. With my non-profit campaign, The Female Lead, I decided early on that we should use the Power of Two to help address the cyclical nature of gender inequality.

Inequality between women and men is still prevalent and pronounced. And following the Covid-19 pandemic, we are going backwards. I attend many meetings throughout the year, talking to corporations or business leaders, and often they will question whether inequality still exists. They will point to more women attending university than men and hold this as a symbol of the battle having been won. They cannot see any further than this.

But, of course, the problem doesn't end there as only 7% of CEOs in the largest publicly listed companies in the UK are women.[2] Therefore, these university degrees are not translating into top jobs or even equal pay in the jobs women secure with their degrees. The barriers, such as caring for families or relatives, are real and tangible for women. Even with a university education, they do not pass through the corporate system to the level they would if the world was equal.

This is also taking a narrow view of what women want because one win does not solve the problems of everyone. For some women, a university education is what they aspire to; for others, it is not something they would like to do. I'd also like to make it clear that when I say 'women', I include all those who identify as women.

Before picking up this book you might not have heard of me, and it is more likely you would be aware of the non-profit campaign I founded, The Female Lead. In the business world, I am known for being one of the pioneers of the Tesco Clubcard, which is one of the first loyalty cards, but my work on The Female Lead is just as important, and I am glad it is about other women and not me. The project itself is an example of what can happen when the micro changes into the macro because we are strong when we stand and use our voices together. It is what happens when, as individuals, we push for the changes we want to see by beginning firstly with ourselves and gradually rolling them outwards. This is the process we shall explore throughout these chapters, alongside the commonalities there are among the Female Leads' choices, approaches and outlooks. We want to know how they developed their self-belief to step into the centre of the room and remain there.

Strength comes from knowing who we are, and this brings self-confidence and self-belief. When we know who we are, we can start to create a plan – and a plan starts to give us power. We begin with the self in the first part of the book, where we look at what is important to us and where our true talents lie. We then consider the areas of fulfilment and the key concerns within these areas for women, before branching out past the societal, economic and geographic barriers women face into the macro decision-making roles of governmental and economic power.

But first, let us begin with the power of data and stories, how they were fundamental in my life and ultimately led to the creation of The Female Lead.

In 1951, only 34.7% of working-age women in the UK were employed. This had only increased by 0.5% since 1931.[3] By 2023 that number has doubled to over 72%.[4]

THE POWER OF DATA

I first came across the unique insight data can provide when I joined an American software consultancy firm in the early eighties, which had opened up a new London branch. At 22, I was hired as a 'Girl Friday', a twee name of its time for a secretarial and administrative assistant. I had just finished a stint in secretarial college after completing a geography degree. Back then, most women's job opportunities were usually limited to either secretary, nurse, waitress or teacher. I had daydreamed my way through school as it didn't ever light a fire for me and, fortunately, there wasn't much secretarial work at my new job, so I could emerge from the back room and see what was happening out at the front.

The company I had joined, Californian Analysis Centres Inc. (CACI), was revolutionary in its approach to data and also its employees. The business was entrepreneurial by nature, and therefore there wasn't the strict hierarchy found in so many companies back then. Right from the start, I learned that if you wanted something to happen, you had to make it happen. You had to be in charge, direct your efforts, build on success and overcome failure. I was encouraged to take risks. It was one of the original start-ups. Consequently, they looked past the role I had been hired for and began exploring where my natural talents lay.

Like many women born at the same time as me, my childhood was held within a small circle that revolved around my family. As middle-born children often realise, I had to find a role for myself within my family dynamics. I wasn't the gifted firstborn or the funny, sweet baby. Instead, I felt I was the slightly nondescript middle one who decided that listening and mediating would become some of her skills. I wanted to understand those around me and realised I could do that twice as quickly by listening to them rather than talking at them. By listening to others, I learned the skill of problem-solving through understanding people and what drove and motivated them.

Shortly after I began working at CACI, they hired a new economist who had developed a way of classifying people and neighbourhoods called 'ACORN'. He needed an assistant and I jumped at the chance. This was when I was introduced to the raw power of data. ACORN was a forerunner of the MOSAIC classification that underpins much data analysis and credit scoring. At school, I had struggled to focus on homework, but when it came to my work and evangelising about data, I had no problem at all. I learned how to read data, understand its outcomes and make it create value for businesses.

Together, the data scientist and I would barrel around the country, sometimes to five meetings a day, preaching a new approach of sorting and describing people into 38 different categories to every bank and building society that would meet with us. For the first time, we could use aggregated census data to tell banks and businesses what kind of people lived within a quarter-mile radius of their store or branch. The creator of ACORN was a brilliant pioneer but, like nearly all data scientists, he wasn't a very good communicator. He could produce data but struggled to translate that into the benefits of the system and how they could be activated. However, I understood the benefits, *and* I could read the data. I couldn't do the deep maths behind it, but I could communicate how the data could be used and interpret the outcomes. I knew I could walk into a meeting room and explain to a manager that if they knew the type of people who lived in an area, they could tailor their products to meet those people's needs and turn them into customers. I also knew the value of this work and wasn't scared of asking for its worth in payment.

So, I took a risk and suggested that I spoke when we were in the meetings. He agreed and I focused on becoming an expert in communicating data's benefits. I built up a client base, hired people to assist me and by the time I was 26 years old I was managing a team of 45. I was growing up fast, and I loved it.

I had begun working in a niche area of data with another data scientist, Clive Humby, who was my polar opposite. Working together, we really learned about the Power of Two. Initially, it isn't easy to spend so much time with someone who thinks differently from you, does things differently and has a different style and way. But it's immensely powerful. There is a huge element of trust to it, but by working with your polar opposite, you are stronger and can go further than you would do apart. Through all those hours spent working side by side, Clive and I fell in love and married. Our mutual respect for each other's skills has kept our marriage strong for 40 years.

The department Clive and I created together began as a small part of a big company, and from there, we just grew. We wanted to process data in a way that had never been done before and, to do this, we needed the most advanced computer centre. Computing power in those days translated into size – it was huge. To get it into our office, we arranged to close one of the main roads in Holborn on a Sunday so it could be craned inside. It was the biggest in commercial use and only rivalled by the Ministry of Justice and the Meteorological Centre. But with our new state-of-the-art monolith of a computer, we could produce maps overlaid with graphics. These clearly showed footfall to a building society that didn't know where to put their next cash machine, or which branches to close or open by using automated data and insight for the first time. By providing something visual, businesses could understand these things more easily and whether they should open something, close it, build on it or enhance it. By giving them a new perspective on the problem, it made their decision easy. This is what data can do.

When Clive and I married, I experienced something that would test me and ultimately make me stronger. Shortly after we married, my bosses called Clive into a meeting where they suggested I exit the business – 'phased out' was the phrase they gave it. They explained that they weren't comfortable working with a married couple. Infuriated by the injustice of it all, I turned to data to help me. I called another meeting and told them that I was either in or I was out, but no one was going to *phase me out*. I then showed them data on how much of the business I managed and how much money I had made for them in the past few years. These facts were indisputable. Shortly afterwards, I was told that they were willing to try and 'make it work'. I could stay as long as I used my maiden name, so it didn't appear that we were married.

After that, I had a new level of drive that I had never experienced before. When we are treated unfairly, it can motivate us, give us an edge that we never knew we had. Clive and I continued with our unique area of data and worked our way up, with Clive eventually heading up the business and me running the most valuable teams.

Overnight, everything changed when our American bosses decided that someone British couldn't lead in the UK, and they shipped in someone from the USA. We now had to report to a new person who came from a legal background. This person cared little about our work – all they cared about was the bottom line. The joy we had experienced in our projects for the previous nine years dropped away because this manager was a cost-cutter and was stripping out the profits from our side of the business each year to help the American side. Suddenly, we had gone from working in an energised, entrepreneurial and revolutionary company to one focused solely on saving money.

Clive and I approached the American bosses and asked them to invest in a new idea we'd had that we thought would solve any financial problems they might have. For the past decade, we had only been working with census data that was now 10 years old. We wanted to change that to working with customer data. We had been thinking about all the things we could do with this data: not only could you understand where people lived, but you could also understand where your *customers* lived. We believed this was where the data market was heading, and we wanted to jump ahead of it. At the time, this was revolutionary. No one had really considered it before, and businesses were throwing away customer data as it was too expensive to own the computing power to store it. It's difficult to imagine now, but all around the country companies were deleting their customer data every three months. We knew the first step would be to invent a way to compress this data so businesses could store it.

We thought this was a brilliant idea – CACI did not and refused to find the investment funds or leave us with the profits we had generated to cover it. We were both dismayed at their decision as we were certain it was the future of data. Clive handed in his notice and took our idea with him. We had agreed that I would remain so he could take some time to think about what he wanted to do and, with me still working, we could cover the mortgage payments on our new home.

Around 10 minutes after Clive resigned, I was fired. I was informed that they didn't want a mole in the camp. They couldn't do it now, but employment law was much laxer at the time. So, in short succession, we were both out of work and up to our eyeballs in debt owing to our new mortgage. All we could do was set up a business from our kitchen table and quickly find a client. Clive began working out how to compress the data and I began hunting for a client. I soon won us a project with Booker Cash and Carry, who wanted to know the type and number of products they should stock for each of their stores. They were wholesalers, so we had to use data to pinpoint where other businesses were that would buy from them. This would test us, as collecting data on other companies rather than people was something new because we couldn't rely on census data, but we were confident we could do it. We built a database of schools, pubs and small restaurants that shopped there and looked at the supply and demand by catchment areas. It was one of the first of its kind and was used for years afterwards in the market.

Everything was looking up when a letter dropped through our door. Our old company had issued a writ against us in the High Court, and we were barred from working until it had been resolved. CACI claimed we'd stolen our new technique from them, and we had to argue that we had invented it. We fought that case for three months, all the time knowing that if we lost the case, our fledgling business would collapse under the weight of our old bosses trying to crush us. We also had to find some big funds for expensive lawyers. Finally, in 1989, the High Court ruled for us. At 30 years old I was finally free to decide how I wanted to run a business.

What I hadn't factored in was that I would be building a business with a new baby to look after as well. Technically, I was the boss. But as a start-up entrepreneur with just two of us, I was also the boss of nothing. If I didn't do the work, it wouldn't get done. Much juggling ensued, and I was lucky that when we rented a small office, it was just down the road, so I could get home quickly if I was needed.

We soon built the pioneering database we had been dreaming about for over a year. We wrote a business plan (which turned out to have no connection to what we finally ended up doing – which is often the way) and started working with companies with a lot of customer data.

It went well, and our kitchen table business grew. As CEO, I was in charge of negotiating all our deals and managing all our staff. I believe that to truly reach our full potential, we firstly have to acknowledge our strengths. One of my strengths is recognising where this lies in others, and I firmly believe there is greatness in everyone. To build our business, I used this skill every day, hiring the outliers who I had a good feeling about, or giving employees a chance to change roles and play to their strengths.

Around five years later, Tesco approached us as they had a problem they couldn't solve by themselves. They had been testing the concept of a reward card, which no other business had done before. The problem they had encountered was that they had so much data none of their software could process it. At the time, the only tool available to process data was spreadsheets, and their data was so large it literally didn't fit into the spreadsheets. They asked us if we would like to do a sample analysis of their data from around nine stores. What could we ever say to that, apart from – yes! We processed their data incredibly quickly and produced the report to the person from Tesco who had approached us. After reading it, he realised that his bosses would have many questions and invited us into the boardroom to explain what we had done. We gathered our data and prepared our presentation for the biggest meeting of our careers. I remember thinking at the time how strange it was that only a few years earlier I had been working on a supermarket till as a teenager and now I was presenting to the board of Tesco. At the end of our presentation, the CEO, Ian MacLaurin (now Lord MacLaurin), sat back and said, 'You know more about my business after three months than I know after 30 years.'

This was all the confirmation we needed.

Of course, MacLaurin was being modest about his knowledge of his business, but he was an incredibly clever man and recognised that data could process and track spending habits more efficiently and accurately than even the most experienced of retailers. Things moved quickly after that. The data we produced proved that by giving customers a reward they returned to you. This was ground-breaking as people don't usually shop exclusively at one supermarket, but by providing a reward, they will visit you one more time. What was particularly revolutionary about the concept was that the customer data tailored the reward to the items you wanted to buy. Before that, there might have been money off nappies in the store, but if you didn't have a nappy-wearing child, what use was that to you? Or they might reward you by swapping one brand for another, such as Pepsi trying to lure away Coca-Cola drinkers with money off their product. What we were saying was, if you like Coca-Cola, have some money off Coca-Cola by using your points.

Tesco decided to bet everything on this loyalty card, which they had named the 'Tesco Clubcard', and organised a national rollout within only a few months. It was the first of its kind, and they had placed immense trust in us and the fact that our data was accurate and the risk was worth taking. Its potential to fail is difficult to imagine now as most large retailers have this type of reward scheme, but at the time it was a nail-biting experience. On a Sunday night in 1995, Tesco closed every store, dressed them all with Clubcard signage and launched their TV advertising campaign. They spent £150 million on advertising and the launch, and it would have significantly changed their fortunes if it hadn't worked. If it hadn't, we might all be shopping at Walmart now. Of course, it did work because Tesco is now the largest supermarket retailer in the UK, and it achieved this status within a year of the launch and doubled its market share within three years. It is generally accepted that the Clubcard was the most pivotal moment in Tesco's trading history.

The project had been a resounding success and we decided to take our new way of processing data to the global market. As the cofounder and CEO, it was my job to travel the world and sell our services to the largest corporations in existence. Clive and I had an agreement that one of us would always remain in the UK with our two children. This meant that I would often walk into a boardroom by myself – and all the people who would turn to face me were men. Nothing I experienced in my past had prepared me for that. I wasn't the finance director, I wasn't Chief People Officer or Head of HR, I was the CEO, the representative for our entire company, and there were no other female CEOs or board members around me. I was also still in my early forties, so I was usually much younger than everyone else as well. Negotiating with these multibillion-dollar companies, who had reputations as commercial bullies, was down to me.

I approached it by sticking with the facts, as I never forgot the power of data. I told them the truth: 'These are the facts. This is what you need to do.' This sometimes provoked much sucking in of air between teeth, rolling of eyes and attempts at negotiation. I would always talk about how we could make it better rather than tell them what they were doing wrong, so they could focus on the solution we could provide. I had also created a joint-venture model to present to each of them, the basis being, 'If we win, you win'. I had chosen this way of packaging our services because it was a much more robust way of talking to people who were used to winning. It didn't set me up against them. Instead, it reformed our relationship as a partnership where we could both be winners.

Tips: Negotiating with a stronger party

- Start with respect and after having done your homework.
- Be prepared and know who you're dealing with. You should know what their job involves, their responsibilities and the ethos of the business they work for.
- Review what you or your organisation has that they value. What are your strengths and their strengths when entering negotiations?
- Consider the cards that you hold. Are you a rare resource? Is the timing and your ability to react to your advantage? Are you trusted but more costly than your competition?
- Be confident of your skills and credentials but be credible and stick with the facts.
- Lay out the solution you provide professionally and clearly. Make sure they understand all that you are including and guaranteeing.
- Be prepared to reduce some of the scope or options and provide a simpler solution. However, never discount the price arbitrarily, as you will cause friction with your office or team.
- Paint a picture of what could happen if they select your proposal and what they risk if they use someone with less expertise.
- Use confident language, and never make the decisions personal. However, you can make the person you are dealing with the organisation's hero for choosing you.

- Be gracious, even in defeat. How you respond to a definite 'no' defines you as a negotiator. Always end a conversation politely, as there might be an opportunity to revisit it.
- Business is a marathon and not a sprint. People you met years ago might be your most important client in the future.

By the time I was in my mid-forties, I would be travelling from Korea to America, to Canada and on to India in the space of a few weeks. In France, I was affectionately called '*le bulldozer*'. However, despite the fulfilment I found in my work, my body rarely knew which time zone it was in. After 10 years of this, we were ready to sell our company. We made a substantial amount of money and prepared to retire. Data had been the basis of my career for nearly 30 years, and I thought I was finally ready to step away from it.

In 1972, Katharine Graham was the first woman to become a CEO of a Fortune 500 company. Fifty-one years after Katharine Graham broke into the Fortune 500, only 10.6% of these CEOs were female – 89.4% were male.[5]

THE FEMALE LEAD AND THE POWER OF STORIES

So how did someone who has worked with data all her life and is best known for being one of the pioneers behind the Tesco

Clubcard end up creating a non-profit, community-led movement aiming to break the societal cycle of gender roles? The two might not seem to fit together on paper, but they are actually very similar. In both cases, we take a lot of people and share the distinctive patterns they create. With the Tesco Clubcard, we focused on the demographics of shopping patterns. With The Female Lead, we compile the concerns of women and what fulfils them, and research specific topics such as the effect of social media on teenagers, hybrid working and women at work.

However, there is one key difference between the two halves of my career – stories. When it came to The Female Lead, stories were where it all began on that small corner desk in our attic-room offices, as it was partly inspired by my own personal experiences. After working in the business world for so many years and having walked into hundreds of boardrooms with no women in them, the inequality hit home on a daily basis. When it comes to the people running the largest corporations in the world, gender inequality is on clear display. It also made me think about the loss of potential. Where were all the women who should have been sitting in those rooms adding their voices? What were they doing instead?

I am sure most women have experienced being underestimated by a man, and this has followed me throughout my career from Girl Friday to CEO of a billion-dollar company. It's exhausting to constantly fight to prove yourself, and I experienced this in my social life too. In the early years of the business, if I told someone at a party that I had started a company with my husband, I would often be asked if I did the books for him when, in reality, I was leading all the commercial discussions. By the end of my career, I was regularly asked why I still worked. I was told I had a lot of money and could therefore afford to stop working. Would anyone have asked a man in my position the same question? Or would they have asked him what his next ambition or goal was?

To begin with, only three of us worked on The Female Lead, and we knew that stories and data should be at the heart of what we did. Stories have always helped me understand people and their motivations. They've helped me become a problem-solver. To this day, I still believe there is a large divide between people who understand numbers and people who can communicate stories. So often, we throw numbers at a problem when really, we have to share the narrative, which often leads to a better under-standing than data can provide. It was why we brought the two together, so we could reach as many people as possible. It is also why I have woven some of the hundreds of stories collected from the Female Leads we've interviewed over the years into this book. They are the lifeblood of The Female Lead and add both connec-tion and colour.

When I first set up The Female Lead, I funded everything myself but aimed to make it into a self-supporting foundation that was an independent entity. I knew it would only achieve this if it was a viable project and deemed valuable by other organisations that would eventually help to sponsor it. We knew it was a worthy objective, but the path to its execution was not initially a smooth one (they rarely are). Our thoughts originally began with a film – we would make a film about women. This idea quickly went into the waste basket when we realised that writing film scripts was not something we could just pick up and run with unless we wanted the end product to be horribly cheesy. So we switched to a docu-mentary before finally settling on a book, *The Female Lead: Women Who Shape Our World*. The book aimed to show teenage girls in schools that there was a whole world of role models out there, not just the ones that algorithms would deliver to them on social media. The book would be a compilation of the stories of inspiring Female Leads, and we would eventually distribute it to 18,000 schools in the UK and America.

We thought we would do a book, and that would be the end. But as is so often the case, one thing led to another, and the book turned out to be just the beginning, not the end. Next, we made some short films, all the time not quite believing how far we had come. The more we did, the more women approached us with their experiences of unfairness and imbalances, and we had to decide whether we were just going to help teenage girls or women at every stage. This gradually extended our work agenda, and at the same time, academics began to come to us with their research. We were receiving all this brilliant research, but none of it was being used or shared. Our reach finally entered the stratosphere when we hired someone to run our social-media campaigns, and off the back of that initiative, we were able to start our own research projects. The best way of describing how we reacted to our successes was that they surprised us – the team was always in a place of mild to extreme surprise at what we achieved. What had once been a single activity became multiple interests and demands.

From the first book to the latest media campaign, we have kept individual stories at the heart of what we do. Without them, there wouldn't be The Female Lead. We simply help by amplifying women's voices through our social-media reach and aggregating them to produce data.

When it comes to the data side of The Female Lead, we are building towards collecting the opinions of around 200,000 people who are predominantly women. What sets data apart from stories is that we're never interested in one person, as that doesn't give a breadth of opinion. We're pretty interested in 1,000 opinions and very interested in 100,000. The data we currently have is larger than any similar collection in the UK. We also have nearly 8 million followers across all our social-media channels. That's almost 8 million people who recognise that inequality is still in existence and are adding their voice by choosing to engage with the women who we help amplify. That's a number and an opinion that governments, politicians and lawmakers can't ignore.

We still need the data side of The Female Lead as it provides irrefutable proof for an essentially male leadership in most decision-making roles. Data also avoids emotions, which are often dismissed or ridiculed. Data can also provide solutions. If enough voices are saying the same thing, we have crowdsourced wisdom. Ultimately, this crowdsourced wisdom will determine where we concentrate our efforts because it is the many that deliver insights on what the majority believe is right and fair.

There is something else that needs explaining about the data we are dealing with at The Female Lead. It's a bottom-up strategy, not top-down. Some organisations will survey and ask questions to test a thesis, to try and prove it works or to gather information on a narrow group of people. Neither of these would produce as accurate results as the type of data we are gathering. With our data, we take all the individual components and keep adding them up in different ways. As a result, we identify themes and bands of people with similar concerns. It's this type of data that provides enlightening results, rather than trying to prove an invented, biased theory.

The reason that individual stories are still so important to The Female Lead is that when we see someone with a similar background to us achieving something, it becomes a possibility for us. Suddenly, something happening way off over there is a possibility for *me*. The power to succeed in our unique ambitions is within all of us, but often it has to be sparked by witnessing it in others. Seeing really is believing. This allows us to recognise it in ourselves – at least the potential – and then we can nurture it. Therefore, stories can cross barriers in a way that data can't always do.

It wasn't until 1967 that contraception was available to all women on the NHS. Prior to this, it was only accessible through this route if pregnancy carried a risk to the woman's health.

COMMONALITIES OF THE FEMALE LEADS

Everything we do at The Female Lead is to encourage people to take the lead in their own lives and explore how others have done this. It is a community of connectivity, and providing a broad range of role models is part of that. It is then the individual's choice if they want to emulate some of those attributes and actions. We have interviewed hundreds of pioneering women for articles for The Female Lead and have noticed commonalities between them and the routes they took. In all cases, taking the Female Lead begins with ourselves. This is the time to think about what inspires us, who we are and our needs, and celebrate those around us.

Part I covers this and is broken down into three main steps:

1. Become inspired

When we see what others have achieved, it opens up doors in our minds that were previously closed. Choosing our role models is not about copying someone else. Instead, we select a little of one person, a sprinkling of another, and so on, until we create our own unique Female Lead that we want to become.

2. Know yourself

This is about understanding what fulfils us rather than pursuing something we have been told we should chase. It is about being the best version of our true, authentic selves, and we can only do this if we work towards what naturally motivates us.

3. Celebrate strengths

This is about acknowledging what makes us special and where our strengths lie. Everyone has these, but they need to be recognised and nurtured. We also need to avoid comparing our weaknesses with others' strengths, as this is not a level playing field. Finally, we celebrate our differences and view others with mutual kindness and respect.

Part II then moves on to the six areas where women find fulfilment. Not all women are the same, and not all of their needs are the same. By using data, we can pinpoint key areas women are concerned about and where change is needed. Once you have a large number of contributors, you have commonalities and can describe patterns of behaviour, preferences and positions. There is power in commonalities because when a voice is united with others with similar concerns, it is more likely to be heard. In these areas, there are key concerns for women and, using data, we high-light the areas where they believe change is needed. We also share the stories of inspiring Female Leads so that you know you are not alone in what you are going through. By focusing on the areas of fulfilment that are important to you, you can prioritise your needs before considering how far you want to go in impacting the communities around you.

Finally, Part III ends on the macro level of economic and decision-making power. This is where the data shows the clearest inequalities between men and women. These areas are crucial for overall gender equality because governments and large corporations drive decisions at a societal level, and until they represent their populations, they will not consider all concerned. We also consider what the world would look like if women had half of those decision-making roles – if we were truly *in the room*.

You might wonder whether we can solve all the problems we face and ever reach true equality. I believe we can solve problems a bit better over time and keep on doing this for as long as we can. So often, governments and large organisations force people into binary decisions – we are only presented with two alternatives, which is a hard construct. But people often see the world in a kaleidoscope of different ways to approach these problems, and that's why I believe in crowdsourced wisdom to highlight the best ones. These three steps of self, fulfilment and macro have been my journey too.

From what I've seen and learned, the best way to approach a problem is to begin with yourself: know who you are, what you believe in, and align yourself with a community and have the strength of the community with you as you go through that process. It's not about a single truth or a single rightness. And one size never fits all. Instead, it's about self-knowledge and alignment with what you trust and believe in. This all begins with the self, where our journey will now begin.

> In 2022, of the top executives at S&P 500 companies, women only controlled about 1% of the value of shares held among fellow leaders.

PART I

EMPOWERING WOMEN ON THE INDIVIDUAL LEVEL

CHAPTER 2

BECOME INSPIRED

There is something magical that happens when young girls meet their heroes. For months we filmed children and teenagers just before or while they met someone they admired. Returning to them a few years later, we interviewed them about the experience. The research gathered from this shows that the impact of meeting a hero or role model results in more self-belief and more confidence because suddenly, these girls feel special. It opens up their world. They have been singled out to meet an amazing woman, which changes them. It is an experience that signals their value and this honour can't be taken away. It's not a short-term effect and, instead, creates long-lasting change. Amazing things really do happen when girls meet their role models.

I met my first role model when I joined CACI. Her name was Mel, and she was in her late twenties. I had never really been fully engaged or motivated at school, and I wasn't sure what I would find in the world of work. Mel wasn't my direct boss, but she was more experienced and senior than me. I looked up to her in those early days – what she did and how she did it. She was generous and let me shadow her. Mel had an energy about her that I admired. She was clearly very clever, but what struck me was how she made her work fun. She showed me that it was possible to excel in your career, be respected by your colleagues, but also bring so much joy and pride to the process. Meeting her changed my whole perspective on work. From her, I learned that you can enjoy yourself while at work and being around your colleagues. You can combine laughter with proficiency.

The idea behind meeting or hearing from our role models is a powerful one as we learn by seeing. Witnessing someone we admire doing something makes it possible for us and shows us that there is another way to live our life. It can be harnessed at any age but is particularly transformative for children, teenagers and young adults because this is a crucial period when budding minds are still forming and deciding what they believe about themselves. It is the time when 'I'm not pretty enough. I'm not thin enough, I'm not clever enough' could become part of their beliefs. When you meet a role model who confirms they thought the same things about themselves when they were younger, it shows that these concepts can be overcome.

One of The Female Leads we interviewed is Dr Vanessa Ogden, a passionate and smart headteacher, who organised for her students to meet Michelle Obama. I met one of these students when she was 25 years old, Nusrath Hassan, who told me that she first met Michelle Obama when she was 17 years old for the Let Girls Learn campaign launch. Nusrath had been invited to join Michelle Obama on stage for the launch interview of her book. What stayed with Nusrath was that this world-famous First Lady had taken the time to leave a handwritten note inside a copy of the book for her. It read, *Keep using your voice with pride.* Nusrath took that to heart and it has been at the centre of everything she has been doing since. Nusrath decided to devote herself to serving her community and the school she grew up in. She now uses her voice with pride, just as Michelle Obama told her to.

How do you scale this transformative process so more girls can experience its effects? So many people who don't have access to lucky opportunities, or aren't privileged, never get to meet these people. Michelle Obama and others like her cannot travel around the world meeting every girl who looks up to them. So instead, what we have been working on since the very beginning at The Female Lead is bringing these role models to young girls and boys through video content, social media and, of course, our books. The key to social-media content is to make people as authentic as possible. So instead of airbrushed celebrities, these Female Leads are people who make mistakes, aren't perfect and don't always look like Penélope Cruz.

The Academy Award-winning actor, Geena Davis, beautifully described the effect it has on young girls to view role models in the media. She told The Female Lead:

Media images are a powerful force in shaping perceptions of our value to society. When you see someone like yourself on screen, doing interesting and important things, you get the message: *There's someone like me. I must matter.* The stark gender inequality in media aimed at young children is significant, whether digital, television, movies or gaming, and wields enormous influence on kids who are developing a sense of their role and purpose in our society. And since children watch the same content repeatedly, negative stereotypes get imprinted again and again.

She felt so strongly about the media's role in shaping young people that she founded the Geena Davis Institute in 2004 to work collaboratively with the entertainment industry on gender balance to reduce stereotypes in what we watch and listen to.

I first had access to another way of life when I started a babysitting business at 13. There were a couple of incredibly wealthy families included in the people I worked for, so I had glimpses of their glamorous lives. They would throw lavish parties while I took care of the children upstairs. In a way, it was like being thrown forwards 40 years into the Social Media Era when others' lives are open to view. The difference was that this wasn't social media, so it wasn't a curated version. Instead, I saw and heard all that went on. Inside the beautiful 1970s homes, couples still argued on the stairs while spilling wine on the shag-pile carpet. I admired the surroundings, but I was also aware that they didn't automatically lead to happiness.

Coming from a business background, I have never been a fan of management books that tell us how one individual succeeded. They succeeded because of a myriad of factors that were difficult for everyone else to replicate or even emulate. The stories we collect on The Female Lead are a pick 'n' mix – you can choose the bits you like, the ones that resonate with you and blend them into your own version of what you want to aspire to or learn from. This is important with role modelling. We don't want to *be* another person, such as Laura Bates or Meryl Streep. Instead, we take inspiration from parts of them and blend them into our own Female Lead.

It is this blend of influences that is so important and, logically, why just stick to one person? As the neurobiologist, Dr Cori Bargmann, put it so succinctly in her interview with us:

I've worked with really smart people at every stage of my career, starting with those who advised me when I was a student and going on to the people who work with me now. So I wouldn't pick out one person as my greatest influence - I would say that every day one person makes me think about something in a new way or try something that I wouldn't otherwise have tried.

This idea of having a wealth of women to choose from comes from a place of inclusivity. I spent most of my career working with supermarkets, and there is something for everybody in a supermarket. This philosophy has been taken into The Female Lead - there is a role model for everybody. It is not our job to tell people what they should do and who they should know about. Instead, we want to offer up some elements that could work for all and be respectful of everybody. The wider the choice, the more likely there is a chance of a new viewpoint, and a single idea can change a life.

To attain true self-knowledge, we must first recognise the qualities we admire and what beliefs we buy into. Who or what do we aspire to be? Quite often, this process is more accessible by recognising it in others rather than ourselves. It is also something that can be done at any age. If we can work out what will light a fire under us, it enables us to invest our time in this area of our life and wake up excited each day. The opposite of this is coasting: just waiting for something to happen or living for the weekend or a holiday. It's so easy to get trapped in a single way of living very early on in life and believe that there's no opportunity to change it. We have seen this in our own research on teenagers' use of social media, called *Disrupt Your Feed*. Our study showed that passive use of social media, where people scroll mindlessly through feeds, is associated with more negative emotions. In comparison, active use of social media, where they search for posts that feed their interests, expands the participant's interests and lifts their spirits about schoolwork.

When we are older, it is sometimes easier to name the reasons why life doesn't let us achieve what we wanted to. I've watched some older women meet their heroes and there can be a certain sadness to the occasion. It's almost as if they wished they'd done something differently or believed their chance for change is over. I've also seen many older women completely reinvent themselves, their careers or lifestyles at various stages. Going from data science to being passionate about The Female Lead was a huge transformation in my working life. A decision to change later on in life usually stems from a mindset of refusing to accept what parts of society might be telling us – that we are too old, washed-up or have nothing left to contribute. Deciding to move along a different trajectory is a new era for these women that they can enjoy in a different way. As they say, a change is often as good as a rest, and a change in career or ambitions can often sweep away the weariness that comes with dealing with the same situation day after day, because new challenges and problems to solve can reinvigorate us.

CHOOSING OUR ROLE MODELS WISELY

The direction our life takes comes from the choices we make, whether they are decisive actions or our response to circumstances outside our control. Choosing a role model is something that we should have complete control over and is an active decision. This early step of empowerment will impact the direction we decide to take in life, so it should be done wisely.

When we choose role models, we can select some for their achievements and others for their characteristics. This dual process means that when we see a role model who has done something that we might not be able to do to a similar level, such as being the fastest 100-metre sprinter in the world, we don't have to turn away from them thinking it's a fruitless pursuit. Instead, we look at the qualities they have that we admire, and emulate them. Similarly, we might learn about a role model who has achieved something we want but has different core characteristics from us; for example, they are an extrovert whereas we are an introvert. Again, instead of thinking we cannot achieve this ambition, we decide to do it in our own way using our innate qualities because there is more than one pathway to each destination.

Tips: Choosing our role models wisely

- So much of what we admire and want to emulate is encapsulated in what people do and how they do it, rather than how they look.
- Select aspects from different role models you admire rather than trying to replicate another person.
- Choose some role models for characteristics you want to encourage in yourself and other role models for what you want to achieve.
- Try not to be captivated by the qualities you don't have and instead build on and expand your strengths.
- Once you see it, you can be it.

When choosing a role model, whether for their characteristics or achievements, we must feel passionate about them. They should be the sort of person who resonates with us. When they speak, we want to listen. When they are interested in something, we want to learn about it, too. In essence, we believe that they are remarkable. It's also about, recognising what makes us feel good, what fills us with hope about our future and aligning ourself with someone with a similar outlook. Even though we may never meet them, these role models should make us feel like we are not alone and we can stand beside each other while striving for the same thing.

Working out the balance of qualities can take time and shouldn't be rushed. It's about seeing beyond the superficial and not just being captivated by the qualities we don't have. The person who holds those is actually our opposite, and here we can rely on the Power of Two. For example, if we find managing and motivating a team challenging, then we should partner with someone who can do this. Or if we struggle with maths or engineering, we should find someone naturally gifted in these areas. The Power of Two draws on everything that we are not. What is essential is that even though our skills are opposite, we are still united in our core values and ambitions. These will set the direction we take together and continue to unify us when our partnership is tested, as all long-term partnerships are at some stage.

Selecting our role models wisely can therefore apply to a partner we might choose in work or life. This is crucial because our chosen partner changes the outcome more than anything else. We therefore have to think not only about where we want to work but *who* to work with. This philosophy can be extended to the people we surround ourselves with. They will either pick us up when we doubt ourselves or, at our lowest moments, leave us there on the ground. I was once on a panel for Disney with the film director and screenwriter, Ava DuVernay, as she talked about the film she had directed, *A Wrinkle in Time*. When we interviewed her at The Female Lead, she talked about her experiences of making her first film and the impact of the people around her:

I didn't grow up around artists, and I don't come from a family of artists. I started with documentaries, because I thought it would be safe to start with something I knew. *This is The Life*, my very first film, chronicled a little-known arts scene that was thriving in the place where I was from. I was part of the hip-hop generation, really loving what the music was expressing. It felt like it was speaking to and for me. All the people in the scene I knew personally, so I was able to get some great interviews and great footage. It was a remarkable experience. I had people around me who really wanted me to succeed, so it was a warm experience and a good first effort – and from there I was hooked.

The feedback from the Female Leads we have interviewed is that people who are naysayers or who make us feel less about ourself won't help us achieve our life's purpose. The damage they can do is often insidious and will slowly erode our self-worth and self-belief. The advice is to disentangle ourself from them so that we are not overcome by the thought patterns of people who make us feel small.

When looking for qualities we want to emulate, they should be ones that we can see in ourselves. They might be underdeveloped or undiscovered, but they should resonate. We will cover this in Chapter 3, where we will explore how to determine what motivates and fulfils us.

KNOW YOURSELF

What is at the heart of being a Female Lead? Without question, it is knowing yourself. Like choosing a role model, this is an active step. We are choosing to learn about ourselves rather than waiting to be chosen. As women, we have to be the change and put ourselves first – not in a selfish way, but in a way that releases our power and energy. We will consciously move towards this when we choose to put ourselves first. Dr Terri Apter, a psychologist we work with closely at The Female Lead, aptly describes self-awareness and its importance as:

What do I really want? What do I really feel? Who do I want to be? These questions are far more difficult to answer than we may think, yet sound answers are crucial to sound choices. Self-awareness allows us to see the deep implications of our values, to critique our goals, and to reach out and meet the person we want to become.

There is a phrase that I dislike, which is 'finding our other half'. To have a fulfilled life, we must be a *whole* person. We must know who we are and what we stand for before we can consider meeting another person, or people, who accept us for what we are and encourage us to be more all of the time.

To be the best version of ourselves, we have to be our authentic selves. This is the first part of self-knowledge. This rock-solid foundation will set you on your path, guide you along the way and support you in the face of adversity. Without knowing who you are, what drives you and what fulfils you, you will often fluctuate between different goals, ambitions, friendship groups, partnerships and causes. Self-knowledge is the basis of confidence, and confidence is what we need to achieve the seemingly impossible. As neuroscientist and clinical psychologist Professor Ian Robertson says, 'If you have confidence, it can empower you to reach heights you never thought possible. But if you don't, it can have a devastating effect on your future. Confidence lies at the core of what makes things happen.' Perhaps unsurprisingly, it is also one of the key areas that women struggle with.

In a recent poll on LinkedIn, we asked, 'Which topics would you like to explore in our women's leadership course?' We received 22,624 votes and the responses were:

- Confidence and imposter syndrome: 38%
- How to be seen and heard: 30%
- Negotiating skills: 20%
- Emotional intelligence: 12%

The second part of self-knowledge is understanding our strengths and weaknesses. When we are clear about where our strengths lie we utilise them in the best way. If we are great at public speaking, this is how we communicate our message. If the written word is where we are more comfortable, we practise it and turn it into our craft. We also shouldn't ignore our weaknesses as they can always be improved. We might never excel in an area of weakness, but being aware of shortcomings is the key to finding our Power-of-Two partner if this is something we want.

Difficulties in one area can also produce extraordinary results in another. I'll never forget when Jo Malone told us that she attributes her success as a perfumer to her dyslexia. She had never taken exams or finished school, but felt that dyslexia had been her best friend. She explained that people with dyslexia often think outside the box because they can't do things in a conventional way. Therefore, when she looks at business problems, she always thinks of the less obvious solution. She also creates fragrance in the same way – by always looking for the bit that's different.

Some of us are born with the skill of self-knowledge. However, for the majority, we often use feedback from others to form our beliefs about ourselves with varying degrees of accuracy. This is very common and can even turn into a self-fulfilling prophecy if the message is repeated enough times. The challenge is to strip these away to reveal the core, which should be done objectively. It is often difficult to truly know ourself without objective outside input.

Sometimes there are hints of where we truly belong by how we react to our surroundings. When we interviewed Shazia Mirza, she told us about her indirect route to being a comedian. She used to watch a lot of comedy on TV at home, but the comedians were always white men, so she didn't think that was something she could do. So, instead, Shazia studied biochemistry, even though all she wanted to do was drama. It was when she became a science teacher in a school in the East End of London that she began pulling on all her resources to keep 30 boys interested in science. Shazia was 21 years old at the time and mainly teaching 16-year-old boys. She didn't want to be there and neither did they, so she tried to keep their interest by being entertaining. After a while, she realised she was doing standup. She was getting up in the morning and just trying to be funny, which eventually ushered her into a life of being a comedian.

Knowing yourself is also essential for helping to develop relationships, whether at work or in your personal life. Everyone we meet will come with a different motivation and way of interacting with us, which is why we just have to be ourself. We can't keep on changing for different people. Instead, we should be open to being discovered, understood and even teased about our particular quirks.

Learning about myself and my strengths and weaknesses was a journey of discovery, and most of it happened through my work. I certainly wasn't fully formed when I began my first job. I wasn't clear about what I was capable of or how good I could be. It took time to learn about myself and realise that in a great team, no one had the same skills, and each individual filled a gap and made the team stronger. Everyone had their place and won respect.

We learned more about ourselves when we were given anonymous feedback from colleagues. The company I worked for took this very seriously. Their people were seen as their biggest investment, and they wanted to ensure they were getting the best out of everyone. Inevitably, this was a challenging process, but it was interesting to hear what we were good at and what we needed to approach differently. It's not easy to have a mirror held up to you, but that honest feedback enables you to see yourself through other people's eyes.

That process of discovery accelerated even faster as I climbed higher in the business, and psychometric testing became part of interviews for promotions and new roles. This formal feedback often confirms what you already know. But it also gives a shape, a name and a language to the things you might have previously taken for granted. It was a solid foundation for increasing self-awareness and development.

The Female Lead has developed a Fulfilment Finder survey, with the input of psychologists, neuroscientists and coaches, which focuses on Six Pillars of Fulfilment which are important to women's happiness:

1. Self
2. Relationships
3. Health
4. Work
5. Money
6. Society

The survey helps us to understand what fulfils us and where our strengths and weaknesses might lie by identifying which of the personas we are. Fulfilment is so important because it is different from happiness. No matter how happy we are, it is followed by ordinary or even monotonous moments. Fulfilment is about having a higher purpose. Once we know what this is, we can focus on that area and channel our resources towards it. Fulfilment is a long and lasting challenge, encompassing a set of targets or beliefs, and we feel fulfilled when we progress towards that goal. When women's needs are met on this level, their confidence increases, and their ability to expand into the areas of decision-making and economic influence on the macro level increases.

Tips: Becoming more confident

- Know what you are good at. Find out where your strengths lie and focus on these.
- Have a big, bold overarching plan that incorporates where you are and where you want to finish, as well as what you need to learn and do to achieve it. Not many people are remembered for the little things. Instead, they are remembered for big, bold, brilliant achievements.
- Pick the right team or working partnership to complement your strengths.
- Surround yourself with people who make you feel good about yourself and will remind you of what you are good at.
- Encourage your curiosity because curiosity feeds growth.
- Continue to invest in your ideas and big, bold plans. This doesn't even mean financially. It can be an investment of time, resources or commitment.
- Often it is not the case that women lack confidence. Rather, they are usually realistic about their capabilities, whereas men can overestimate their abilities and don't see the limits to their skills or talents, so they often have a higher objective and a bigger, bolder plan as they aren't focused on their weaknesses.
- Confidence is like a muscle; the more you exercise it, the more confident you become. You have to believe in yourself to grow self-confidence.

THE TWELVE PERSONAS

If we can find out what drives us, matters to us most and how we rank the balance between work and home life, we can focus on what is important to us. On this basis, and with the help of a neuroscientist, we have identified twelve personas that have been built from what people feel when they're fulfilled.

Different types of people have different emotional drivers that when satisfied make them feel fulfilled. Some people prioritise safety, excitement, connectedness, power, enjoyment or control. Each persona has a primary and a secondary emotional motivator that stem from the following six emotional states and the feelings connected to them (see Figure 3.1):

We built the personas by taking all of the responses to our survey and looking at the different things women experienced

Safety	Excitement	Connectedness
Calm	Adventurous	Accepted
Comforted	Creative	Belonging
Protected	Energised	Connected
Safe	Excited	Engaged
Secure	Inspired	Involved
Supported	Stimulated	Valued
Power	**Enjoyment**	**Control**
Confident	Carefree	Efficient
Freedom	Enjoyable	In control
Independent	Fun	Organised
Influential	Happy	Practical
Strong	Relaxed	Sensible
Successful	Wonderful	Uncomplicated

Figure 3.1. The six emotional states and the feelings connected to them.

when they felt fulfilled. We then segmented them into groups, much like I did with customers back in my Tesco days, but this time with emotions rather than purchasing habits. The survey we created is based on a wealth of neurodiversity data and explores the subconscious. It is therefore designed to be completed very quickly so that you don't start applying logic to the questions but instead use instinct to tap into your subconscious. You can take the free survey at www.thefemalelead.com/fulfilmentfinder. It is designed to be done within seven minutes and is a non-judgemental way of finding out about yourself. If you don't want to take the survey, just reading about the personas below will help. You will likely find that you are drawn to one or two that resonate, and these will likely have the strengths and qualities that you exhibit.

The twelve personas are categorised into four groups and are a way of discovering your emotional drivers. We begin with knowing which of the twelve personas we are so we know our strengths. Later, we will dig deeper into the Six Pillars of Fulfilment (Part II), so we know which areas of our life to concentrate on to feel strong and in balance and which are out of sync, causing us to feel less fulfilled.

Below are the four key groups and the personas within them, including the primary and secondary emotional motivators that drive their fulfilment.

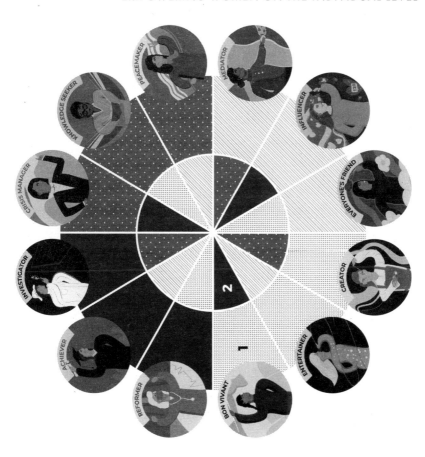

Each persona has two main motivators that drive their fulfilment.

1 Primary emotional driver

2 Secondary emotional driver

The motivators:

Organisers
Love to be in control

Connectors
Need safety and connection

Joy seekers
Seek enjoyment

Leaders
Need power and excitement

ALL-ROUNDERS

All-Rounders are leaders and connectors who organise through and by directing others. The four All-Rounder personas are as follows:

1. **Investigators** are convergent thinkers – people who are able to make clear, logical deductions, given the facts. They are able to think critically and independently. They are likely to be 'news junkies' who need to know what is going on around them. Other people may stereotype them as workaholics, but they are not just  those who put in the hours as they are leaders and problem-solvers as well. They are very practical people who overcome obstacles and tricky situations – the sort of characters in a disaster movie who lead the others out of danger. People turn to them for help to get out of trouble, because they do their homework when solving a problem and find out what the real obstacles are before proceeding.

   Primary motivator for fulfilment: Leaders – need power and excitement

   Secondary motivator for fulfilment: Organisers – love to be in control

2. **Mediators** are social creatures who always seek to get involved with activities with their peers and this contributes to their need to feel valued. Good mediators can empathise well with both sides of an argument. They seek to support and comfort others, but also need to feel supported. They feel  comforted when they win over the confidence of others. They

always seek to understand the feedback others give them but without overly worrying about what others think about them.

Primary motivator for fulfilment: Connectors – need safety and connection

Secondary motivator for fulfilment: Organisers – love to be in control

3. **Influencers** enjoy being with people and bringing them together. Socially, they are very busy, highly visible and approachable. Influencers have confidence in their own abilities and a lot of people look up to them. They may start up their own group or organisation and then bring other like-minded  people with them. Influencers keep moving and creating and won't stand still for long.

Primary motivator for fulfilment: Connectors – need safety and connection

Secondary motivator for fulfilment: Leaders – need power and excitement

4. **Achievers** have an abundance of what psychologists call 'fluid intelligence', which is the ability to examine a problem carefully and apply tried and trusted logical techniques to reach a good solution. They are confident individuals who have built their success on a strategy of hard work, careful planning and making good decisions. That said, they are not afraid to make mistakes. As overtly passionate people, they are able to take people with them and can be persuasive in a friendly way.

Primary motivator for fulfilment: Leaders – need power and excitement

Secondary motivator for fulfilment: Connectors – need safety and connection

CHANGEMAKERS

Changemakers are joy-seekers and leaders who tend to lead from the front with passion and conviction. The two Changemaker personas are:

5. **Bon Vivants** who crave pleasure and success. They exude confidence and strength as they overtly take what they want from life. Sometimes their carefree, relaxed and calm external appearance can hide feelings of anxiety and worry. They are often inspired by ideas that advocate social justice, and in  fighting for a cause they can draw attention to it by daring to be highly visible and different. They would never sell themselves short – they wouldn't lie to hide something about themselves, and are certainly not afraid to call someone out if they are behaving in inappropriate ways.

   Primary motivator for fulfilment: Joy-seekers – seek enjoyment

   Secondary motivator for fulfilment: Leaders – need power and excitement

6. **Reformers** are charismatic individuals, who are confident and strong. As independent people they get their strength from feeling, and being seen to be, successful and influential. As those who

seek the pleasures in life, they do not worry about what others think, and despite the fact that they actively seek to avoid pain, they are certainly not risk-averse. They have had their ups and downs, and know full well that it is okay to make mistakes. They are happiest when championing a cause or

solving a problem – the more adventurous the cause or problem the better.

Primary motivator for fulfilment: Leaders – need power and excitement

Secondary motivator for fulfilment: Joy-seekers – seek enjoyment

GUARDIANS

Guardians are joy-seekers who achieve their goals through strong organisational skills and by connecting with and involving others. The three Guardian personalities are as follows:

7. Creators are those with a lot of originality in the way they think. They are often enthusiasts who are passionate about a particular field or ability. They are likely to really enjoy their work and are not driven by money. As is the case for most things they do in their life, it is clear that they just want

to have fun. However, it is not reckless fun, as they need to regulate how they feel. They are very organised – noticeably so, as things in their home and office are seldom out of place – but there is an original flair in what they do. They probably love DIY or redesigning their home or workplace.

Primary motivator for fulfilment: Joy-seekers – seek enjoyment

Secondary motivator for fulfilment: Organisers – love to be in control

8. Everyone's Friends love social gatherings and seldom turn down invitations to get-togethers because when they feel connected, they also feel safe and secure. They want to feel happy and love to see others happy too. As people with super listening skills and a desire to really  understand how others think and feel, they make great team-builders. Indeed, they feel at their best when they are laughing, having fun and having an exuberant time.

Primary motivator for fulfilment: Connectors – need safety and connection

Secondary motivator for fulfilment: Joy-seekers – seek enjoyment

9. Entertainers are extroverted hedonists, meaning that they seek pleasure and try to avoid pain. Their pursuit of happiness is equated with entertaining others, as well as being entertained by others. Their  enjoyment in the sensory pleasures in life is driven by the need to feel that life is fun and should be about laughing and making others laugh. It's clear to all who know them that they love social gatherings and want to feel like they belong. As leaders or managers, they recognise that it is not about being a good boss but encouraging their team to work towards a collective goal.

Primary motivator for fulfilment: Joy-seekers – seek enjoyment

Secondary motivator for fulfilment: Connectors – need safety and connection

NAVIGATORS

Navigators are organisers who achieve their goals through crisis-management, knowledge-seeking or peacemaking. The three Navigator personalities are listed below:

10. Knowledge-Seekers are voracious readers and logical thinkers, but also seek joy from what they do. They see life as a series of quests or individual, fun-filled challenges that are somehow interlocked. It's not just the practical sense of the here and now that dominates their thinking and brings them joy. They also look to all the possibilities and even fantasies – what might be unthinkable now, but may be possible in the future. The dream of a perfect world motivates them and gives them the ability to concentrate and stay focused on a problem or mission.

Primary motivator for fulfilment: Organisers – love to be in control

Secondary motivator for fulfilment: Joy-seekers – seek enjoyment

11. Peacemakers seek comfort and control in their life. They are more introverted than extroverted and seek an uncomplicated life. They like to comfort others and are a problem-solver and would make an excellent coach or counsellor. They are very practical and highly organised in their life.

They are most likely to be an active member of a club, society or WhatsApp group and are highly motivated to help others. As people who are not afraid to ask for help, they make perfect confidants. They believe that you don't have to do it all alone and that it is better to take someone with you in life.

Primary motivator for fulfilment: Organisers – love to be in control

Secondary motivator for fulfilment: Connectors – need safety and connection

12. Crisis Managers are very practical and could easily survive difficult situations. They are often the first port of call when someone has a personal or even just a practical problem. They are cool, calm and collected, and undeterred when others become aggressive or overly emotional or critical.

Where others would run or shy away from difficulties, a Crisis Manager will face it head on. A lot of their strength actually comes from the admiration others display for their resilience and character.

Primary motivator for fulfilment: Organisers – love to be in control

Secondary motivator for fulfilment: Leaders – need power and excitement

There are also some deep-dive surveys on our website that you could do after this on the Six Pillars of Fulfilment. These will help you explore what matters most to you in each of these critical areas of work-life balance. Our persona changes as we move through life, which has happened to me. I have a dominant persona, but when I was going through a time where I was experiencing a lack of control, my persona swapped into one that was similar but adjacent. Usually though, the persona change will happen in the same group. It's therefore advisable to do the survey again if a significant change occurs in your life, such as starting a new job or ending or beginning a relationship.

WHAT OUR DATA SHOWS ABOUT PERSONAS

We have been collecting data on the most common personas in different categories, and the results are fascinating. They show that not only are there prevalent results in persona types for age groups, but also among countries and other factors too. It reveals how our personas alter as we age due to our changing needs and what we prioritise in life.

The results opposite are taken from data compiled in 2023 from the top twelve countries who have taken our surveys:

MOST COMMON PERSONAS BY AGE

AGES 18–24

Most common persona

(Guardian group)

Second most common persona

(Guardian group)

Most women aged 18-24 are exploring who they are through experiences and connections with others. They are enjoying themselves and generally having fun.

It is also interesting to note that both of the personas fall into the same Guardian group. They are joy-seekers who achieve their goals through organisational skills, and connecting and collaborating with others.

AGES 25–34

Most common persona

(Guardian group)

Second most common persona

(All-rounders group)

Many women aged 25-34 are social creatures, which is reflected in their personas. They are navigating the different types of relationships that begin to develop during this stage of their lives, such as those with their bosses, children and colleagues. In this age group, the Everyone's Friend persona - the second most common in the previous group - climbs to number one. This shows the evolution of the prevalent personas, which continues into the next age group.

AGES 35-44

Most common persona   **Second most common persona**

(All-rounders group)   (Navigators)

By age 35-44, many women feel independent and practical about their lives. They often make decisions for themselves and their families, organising and leading those around them.

Here we have a move away from the joy-seeking Guardian group and a continuation of the leading and connecting All-Rounders. There is also the introduction of the Crisis Manager persona which is known for being practical and able to survive difficult situations (many women in this age group might be nodding their heads while reading this).

AGES 45–54

Most common persona

(All-rounders group)

Second most common persona

(Navigators)

When women reach ages 45–54, many feel more confident and successful. They are often passionate about a cause and can now use their knowledge and experience to achieve their goals.

Interestingly, this is the first age group where the top-ranking personas are exactly the same as the previous one and shows the continuity in the two periods of women's lives. However, there is a difference in the fulfilment pillars for these two age groups, which we cover fully in Chapter 6. At ages 45–54, money is the first fulfilment area, with work as the second. At ages 45–54, work remains the second fulfilment pillar, but the previous first one, money, is replaced by health. This is the first time that health appears in the fulfilment pillars and shows a shift in women's experiences and priorities.

AGES 55–64

Most common persona

(Changemakers group)

Second most common persona

(Changemakers group)

Most women aged 55–64 are now enjoying their influence and are actively focused on the things they truly care about. They can often be found championing a cause, taking the less-trodden path or paving the way for generations to come.

There is a sudden shift in this age group away from the All-Rounders and the Navigators groups and into the Changemakers group. There is a return of the joy-seekers, a trait we haven't seen since the first two age brackets. But this time, as they are Changemakers, they combine this with leadership skills involving passion and conviction.

AGE 65 AND OVER

Most common persona

(All-rounders group)

Second most common persona

(Changemakers group)

Once most women reach age 65 and over, they have more time to enjoy learning new things and take pleasure in that. They are focused on joyful experiences that expand their knowledge and understanding.

As the above shows, our age significantly impacts our persona type, and therefore our persona type will also change throughout our lifetime. Interestingly, our data also shows that the country we live in affects our persona type. This could result from the differing values we are surrounded by. When it comes to the top twelve countries where participants in our surveys live, the data we compiled in 2023 shows:

MOST COMMON PERSONAS BY COUNTRY

We have successfully collected sufficient data from twelve countries, enabling us to analyze women's responses on a geographical level. While a majority of replies come from the UK and USA, we also have substantial data from Ireland, France, Germany, the Netherlands, Switzerland, and Sweden in Europe, along with Australia, New Zealand, Canada, and India.

Each group is further explained below.

ALL ROUNDERS = 37% of women display a wide range of dutiful skills, need connectedness but don't care so much about control or enjoyment.

GUARDIANS = 18% of women thrive on safety, enjoyment and connectedness.

CHANGEMAKERS = 9% of women thrive on power, excitement and enjoyment and are not worried about being in control, safety or connectedness.

NAVIGATORS = 34% of women thrive on being in control and are not so concerned with safety, power, excitement or connectedness.

UNITED STATES: A HARD-WORKING ECONOMY WHERE MONEY MATTERS.

Most common persona

Second most common persona

(All-rounders group)

(All-rounders group)

UNITED KINGDOM: A CULTURE THAT IS COMING TOGETHER FOR A COMMON CAUSE.

Most common persona

Second most common persona

(All-rounders group)

(All-rounders group)

AUSTRALIA: A CULTURE WITH CREATIVE SOLUTIONS TO ECONOMIC PROBLEMS.

Most common persona

Second most common persona

(Guardians)

(The Navigators)

CANADA: A CULTURE THAT CELEBRATES SUCCESS AND VISIBILITY.

Most common persona

(Changemakers group)

Second most common persona

(All-rounders group)

GERMANY: A CULTURE THAT PRIORITISES PLEASURE.

Most common persona

(Guardians group)

Second most common persona

(All-rounders group)

THE NETHERLANDS: A CULTURE THAT PRIORITISES PLEASURE AND VALUES HEALTH.

Most common persona

(Guardians group)

Second most common persona

(Changemakers group)

IRELAND: A CALM, COLLECTED CULTURE THAT BRINGS PEOPLE TOGETHER.

Most common persona

Second most common persona

(Changemakers group)

(All-rounders group)

NEW ZEALAND: A CARING CULTURE THAT PUTS PEOPLE FIRST.

Most common persona

Most common persona

(Navigators)

(Guardians group)

SWEDEN: A CONNECTED CULTURE THAT VALUES INDIVIDUAL CONTRIBUTIONS.

Most common persona

Second most common persona

(Guardian group)

(All-rounders group)

SWITZERLAND: WHERE CULTURAL CHANGE HAPPENS IN CREATIVE WAYS.

Most common persona

Second most common persona

(Guardian group)

(Changemakers group)

INDIA: A HARD-WORKING CULTURE WHERE INFLUENCE AND HEALTH IS KEY.

Most common persona

Second most common persona

(All-rounders group)

(All-rounders group)

MOST COMMON PERSONAS IN OTHER GROUPS

We also collected and produced data on the prevalence of personas in other categories, and which of the six emotional states are driving this, which are shared below:

WOMEN WITH CHILDREN

Most common persona (All-rounders group):

Most women with children living at home are doing it all – they are balancing work, relationships and finances. They are more likely to be mediators, using empathy and understanding to support those around them.

Most of these women want to feel safe as a priority. Feelings of excitement and enjoyment take a back seat while they put their family needs first.

WOMEN WITHOUT CHILDREN

Most common persona (Changemakers group):

Many women without children are taking the less-trodden path. They are confident and seek success, pleasure and influence.

Most women without children feel significantly more enjoyment and excitement than other women. Safety, in contrast, is least important to them.

WOMEN WHO ARE AN ETHNIC MINORITY IN THEIR COUNTRY

Most common persona (All-rounders group):

Many women who are part of an ethnic minority in their country find the majority of their fulfilment through connecting with others. They bring people together and lead with their confidence and creative abilities.

Many women in this situation need to feel in control and place a high amount of importance on that to feel fulfilled. These results are also much stronger than those women who are in the ethnic majority in the country where they live.

SINGLE WOMEN

Most common persona (Guardian group):

Most single women are leaning into new and original ways of doing things. They are passionate, enthusiastic and seeking joy above all else.

Many single women place a lot of importance on feelings of power, which is at similar levels to divorced women. Connectedness and excitement, however, are much less important to them.

MARRIED WOMEN

Most common persona (All-rounders group):

Like women with children, many married women are balancing family life with work and have the same prevalent persona, the Mediator, in common. They use empathy, emotional intelligence and mediation skills to bring connection to those around them.

Many married women feel that connection is most important to their sense of emotional fulfilment. Power, especially in contrast with single women, is far less important to them.

BREADWINNERS

Most common persona (All-rounders group):

Many breadwinners are critical and independent thinkers. As the main breadwinner of their household, they are often very passionate about work and put in a lot of hours. They are natural problem-solvers.

Power and control are very important to breadwinning women. Enjoyment, in contrast, is far less important to their feelings of emotional fulfilment.

WOMEN WITH SHARED FINANCIAL RESPONSIBILITY

Most common persona (All-rounders group):

In contrast to women who are the main breadwinners, women who share breadwinning responsibilities are more likely to be mediators and they place high importance on connecting to and organising those around them.

With shared financial responsibility, many women feel less need for power. Connection and excitement are both a lot more important to these women and safety is of the least concern.

WOMEN WHO AREN'T BREADWINNERS

Most common persona (Changemakers group):

Women who are not breadwinners are significantly more likely to champion a cause or solve a problem. They're happiest when they're enjoying themselves and they want to be successful in their own right.

Women who aren't breadwinners place much more importance on enjoyment and feelings of being in control than feeling power.

WOMEN WHO EARN THEIR OWN MONEY BUT LIVE IN A HOUSE WITH SHARED OCCUPANCY

Most common persona (All-rounders group):

Many women who earn their own money but live in a house with shared occupancy are likely to be Achievers – which means they're intelligent, independent and natural leaders.

They place importance on excitement and enjoyment, significantly more so than other women such as single-income households. Feeling in control is much less important to them at this stage of their lives as they focus on pleasure.

WOMEN WHO USE SOCIAL MEDIA

Most common persona (Guardian group):

Social media seems to make women more likely to be creative. Many of these women are organised yet original in how they approach things. Aesthetics and order are important to them, which could reflect the carefully curated feeds and stories we see on social-media platforms.

Many women who use social media feel less need for control than those who don't use social media. Their need for real connection is most important to them in order to feel emotionally fulfilled.

WOMEN WHO DON'T USE SOCIAL MEDIA

Most common persona (All-rounders group):

Surprisingly, women who don't use social media are more likely to have influencer qualities – bringing people together for a common cause and just for fun. Many of these women are part of organisations or groups they feel passionate about.

Control is most important to women who don't use social media and connection is least important, especially in contrast to those who do.

*   *   *

When we created this persona test a few years ago, I knew it was accurate as soon as my result came up. I was a Reformer. It reflected my attributes and personality exactly. It was no great surprise that I had fallen into the group that was motivated primarily by leadership, but I particularly appreciated that it confirmed that my secondary motivator is seeking joy. This balance between the two has guided most of my pursuits and it was very satisfying to have it confirmed. I only wish I could have accessed it when I was younger, as it would have saved me a great deal of time wondering who I really was.

Now that we have identified our personas, what fulfils us and also where our areas of strength are, it's time to celebrate them and also the strengths of those around us.

CHAPTER 4

CELEBRATE STRENGTHS

When I began my career, and for a long time afterwards, there was a managerial focus on developmental feedback. This meant that when your boss reviewed your work, they would glide over your strengths but then focus on your weaknesses, and these would dominate your self-reflection. You would come out of an annual review session worrying about what you were not, instead of celebrating who you were and what you were naturally gifted at.

Once I got to the position of being the one holding the reviews, I decided to do it another way. Listing people's weaknesses is often a dead end. When someone holds a spotlight on weaknesses, it shifts the person's confidence and focus from where their talents lie. This is counterproductive as you need to build skills and encourage self-belief, not undermine someone at a time of critical development. You also rarely excel at something you are not naturally gifted at. At its best, you can make someone aware of a weakness so they can seek help and partnership, but it shouldn't be what dominates a review. I've never once seen excellence created from a focus on weakness, or seen it produce many worthwhile results in my 30 years of managing teams.

Far more commonly, people excel in areas where they have natural gifts. Therefore, a far better approach is to focus on what someone is really good at and what people love them for. When you are told you are charismatic and can sway crowds or are reliable and consequently everyone depends on you, it makes you grow rather than shrink. So I became an advocate for telling people the area in which they excelled, explaining what would make them even better at it and what would make them the best. It's a 'good, better, best' approach.

This is where celebrating our strengths comes in. Instead of being absorbed by our weaknesses, we choose to focus on our natural abilities. We can then consider what would make us better at them or even the best. We each have special skills, which we potentially undervalue as they come easily to us. Because of this ease, we might even believe that they are not exceptional, but to others they will be. It's about recognising that not everybody finds what you can do easy. That makes you different and strong. Instead of feeling like an imposter, or less than others, you understand that you have a place and a role.

Comparing your weaknesses to someone else's strengths is also not beneficial. Firstly, it isn't a level playing field, and it is unlikely that you will ever be able to improve your weaknesses to match an area in which someone else excels. Secondly, we should celebrate others' strengths without the need to compare ourselves to them, other than using them as a source of inspiration.

We should also try to view all strengths as equal. I was always very good at understanding people and where their skills and motivation lay, but I could never become the expert data scientist that my husband is. If I had focused on my perceived lack of technical skills, I don't think I would be where I am today. Academic skills – or academic failure – too often determine a young person's future. If this is an area that you struggle with, you can always return to learning later in your life, and it doesn't have to be in a formal setting. We can rise at any stage and shouldn't let ourselves be written off or dismissed. There is always a future opportunity for change. If you are unhappy in your current job, it is probably because you are not using your natural talents, either because they haven't been identified or because they don't apply to your role.

OUR COMMUNITY

When we know what inspires us, who we are and our unique talents, our confidence will naturally grow. When we are comfortable with ourselves, we often feel inspired to do something big, and this is when it helps to know what fulfils us. With this confidence, we should do our best to be visible in our achievements, provide inspiration to others and join with them. Trying to identify people we are aligned with in terms of our values, shared interests or causes will help us find others we can relate to – a community.

Women are generally great collaborators, partly because they ask others for help and advice. They shouldn't ever see this as a weakness, whereas some men might think otherwise. Women tend to be very good at giving someone else space to express themselves when in the same room. Collaboration and partnership are often women's superpowers because they're so good at yielding power in a room to allow others to contribute. Sharing space in the room is how women will achieve more than any single man can.

Speaking up and asking for help is a very contemporary form of leadership and a very constructive one. It's transparent and involves shared problem-solving. When we rely on, enjoy and respect each other's strengths, there is forward motion in a positive direction, and we can make progress. When we find our alliances, and those we enjoy working with and who believe in us, our momentum and ability to instil change can grow.

One story that moved me greatly about finding strength in your community and those around you was told to us by Dr Deelan Dakhil Saeed, who is a member of the Yazidi community and works in refugee camps with girls who have escaped from ISIS captivity. She told us that her courage comes from her people.

I was taught courage by a five-year-old child who had to walk for three days without food or water to survive. I was taught courage by each girl I sat with as I heard her story. I never saw the girls as victims: I saw heroes. Every time I had the chance to help them and saw their innocent smiles, I felt confident. And I never forget the people around me who believe in me, who never let me fight alone and who support me. When you don't feel you are alone, it gives you more strength.

Our community can be large or small, and we can belong to several that benefit us in different ways. It might be that we can align ourselves with a community that champions the same cause as us, or with one that makes us feel good about ourselves and gives us purpose.

One of the benefits I received from my work community when I was in a leadership role was the ability to receive feedback. It was scary, but I would ask people for feedback on my performance.

What do you think I'm good at? What is it that you don't like or that worries you? What do I do that makes you feel small? And what makes you grow? It was always nerve-wracking waiting for their answers, but I knew that those dreaded responses would make me grow and improve more than anything else. If you're not scared sometimes, not putting yourself out there, you're probably not growing. Because often the things we don't want to do, because we are scared, propel us forward the most. If you are ambitious and want to excel in an area, you will need the honest feedback of that community of people.

Tips: Asking for feedback

It is natural to fear hearing negative things about yourself or your work, but don't underestimate the power of receiving the positives. When people say constructive things about you, the feeling is overwhelmingly positive and builds your confidence.

In a business setting, anonymous feedback is more beneficial so that you are told the truth. If you ask for people to put their names to the feedback, they will just respond with what they think you want to hear, which doesn't provide any insight.

With anonymous feedback, you might think all you will receive is a series of grumpy responses, but you are much more likely to receive insightful feedback that provides you with a chance to grow. This is because a good team will want you to be successful as no one wants to be associated with failure. This also applies to your team's successes. Too much modesty about your achievements can reflect badly on them and lessens their contribution.

In a non-business setting, you can ask for feedback on an anonymous basis, but it depends on the context. It might be that you limit your request for feedback to the people you would go to for advice. If your community is a supportive one, then this should include most people.

If you find yourself surrounded by people who make you feel less, these probably aren't the type of people you want feedback from. They will likely project what they feel onto you and describe what you are doing as their emotional response to it, such as fear, doubt or anger. Conversely, if someone knows themself and is self-aware, they are much more likely to be an honest judge of others rather than projecting their emotions onto them.

If the idea of joining a large community does not appeal to you, remember that the Power of Two is a type of community as well – a collaborative approach that relies on the polar opposite strengths of two people who are held together by shared values and ambitions. The benefits of this type of collaboration are immeasurable as it's unusual for one person to be able to deliver everything they aspire to. The Power of Two isn't only limited to business settings – history is filled with these incredible unions in all fields, such as Elton John's musical genius combined with Bernie Taupin's poetic lyrics.

It is also incredibly beneficial to have one other person who you can be completely vulnerable with and share your doubts. It is a unifying force because to win, you both have to win as you're in it together. They can also provide you with the most honest feedback because they have known you in weakness and in strength and have often been on your journey from the beginning. They can support and rally around you at your lowest moments and, just as importantly, keep your feet on the ground at your height of success. When you share your power and achievements with someone else, it helps keep your ego in check.

I've been very fortunate to know the Female Lead, Anne-Marie Imafidon, for many years. She has had an illustrious career as a computer scientist and is also the cofounder of Stemettes, which supports and inspires girls, young women and non-binary young people in STEM subjects. Working so closely with young people, she told us, when we interviewed her, that her advice for teenagers is not to do things alone. She explained that you can spend a lot of time trying to learn and discover things on your own and explore on your own. But having people to do that with means that you will probably stick to it for longer, and it will enrich your learning experience. She recommends that young people should find a community, tribe and people to learn things with. That way, they'll have people to answer their questions – and people to celebrate their wins with them.

RESPECTING DIFFERENCES

Once you have found your community, however big or small, you can begin exploring other communities and find common ground with them and where you overlap. You may not align with them on every point, but you can still unite on certain areas. Within your community, you might have strong views and beliefs, but that doesn't necessarily mean that another community is wrong because they are not focused on the same things that you are.

Instead, it means they have a different emphasis, but you can still enjoy or learn from their differences.

As we go through life, we often change communities because as we age, we want and need different things. Our focus shifts to other areas of our life or causes. What fulfilled us when we were 16 might not fulfil us when we are 28, and what inspired us at 39 might not do so at 51. If we know where we are in life, and how this impacts our views, it is easier to respect that others are different because they are experiencing something else. One person's dream is not somebody else's, and we are not all fired up by the same vision. You can't make people think and do as you do because, quite simply, they're not you and they haven't had your life experiences. Mutual regard and respect come down to understanding those differences and not being angered or alienated by them. We focus on what we *do* have in common rather than what we *don't* have in common.

We can also view other communities as a chance to learn. Reaching out for additional pockets of learning is essential at all stages of life. When we contribute to a community or cause, we might even rise to the top of it – leadership is not always in the traditional forms of involvement in a company or business. Wanting to learn about and from others is incredibly important in any leadership role. It is the polar opposite of the narcissistic 'great leader' who proclaims they are wise, experienced, know the answer to everything and their judgement is final. This is a very limiting method of leadership and a dated model as it doesn't allow for innovation or empathy.

When we view other communities with respect, we can start to appreciate the parts we admire and feed this back to them. A genuine compliment costs you nothing, but often there is a reservation that stops us from giving it. But that one thing you say can make a lasting impression and change someone's view of themselves and how the world sees them. I met Maya Ghazal at The Female Lead's second photoshoot in London. She is a Goodwill Ambassador for UNHCR, and the first female Syrian refugee pilot. When we interviewed her, she told us that she wants people to understand that it doesn't take much to make someone's life better. The smallest act of kindness can make a difference. For her, something as simple as someone commenting that her English sounded good made her believe in herself again. Her portrait for our second book – *The Female Lead* (Volume 2): *We Rise By Lifting Others* – is one of my favourites, and reminds me of a subject sitting for a Vermeer painting.

The fundamental point of celebrating strengths is that we have the confidence to use our voice, but the wisdom to know that we don't live alone and shouldn't want to live in a world where we're the only key player. So when we celebrate strengths, we listen and learn at the same time. We listen even to the quiet ones who rarely speak, but when they do, say the most wise and sensible things. So often we are overwhelmed by the loudest voices because dissent, even though there is a lot of it, is very quiet. That's not democracy. That's just fear of being shouted down, which equates to bullying. We don't want to live in a world of bullying-style leadership and decision-making, where the loudest voice wins. This is, in part, why I love the truth and collective wisdom that data produces.

RISE BY LIFTING OTHERS

When we begin to enjoy success, whatever sphere that is in, we have a choice to make. We can either pull up the drawbridge behind us so others can't follow, or we can extend our hand and help them up. When women choose not to help others in this way, it usually stems from fear of there being only a finite quota for women in well-paid jobs. Instead of helping to fix a broken system, they are choosing to accept it. My first role model, who I met at work in my early twenties, was always willing to help me and from a young age, I knew this would be how I would treat the women coming up behind me.

When we interview our Female Leads, time and again we hear that they believe in rising by helping others. These are some of the world's most successful and respected women, and a clear theme among them is that they don't see other women as a threat. Instead, they have seen other women paving the way for their successes and want to do the same in turn. As Nimco Ali, an activist and cofounder of Daughters of Eve, explained to us:

> I don't think of myself as a leader but as part of a chain. If it wasn't for all the amazing women who came before me and the women alongside me, I wouldn't be able to do any of these things.

In turn, this impacts our relationships with the women around us and who we admire. Lady Nicola Mendelsohn, Vice President of Facebook for Europe, the Middle East and Africa, told us that Sheryl Sandberg is the woman who most inspires her because she cares deeply about helping women thrive in the workplace: 'She's not somebody that pulls the ladder up behind her. She throws ladders down because she wants more and more women to succeed.'

How do we react to someone who is utterly brilliant at something we pride ourselves on as one of our strengths? Our initial reaction might be to doubt ourselves, be jealous or pick faults in what they do. These reactions boil down to fear that they will hurt us or take something away from us. Another way of looking at this is acknowledging that their strengths do not degrade your value. Seeing them as someone to aspire to be or even as a potential future mentor is a way of learning from them and using their experience to inform your own life.

Fundamentally, if we want to see more women step into the room, then we, as women, have to help them get there. It benefits all of us. As Elizabeth Nyamayaro, the United Nations Special Advisor for the World Food Programme, says:

My advice is always to lift others as you rise. If you're a woman dealing with intersectional issues, the more you can have people like yourself alongside, the better. The more you normalise people like yourself as you climb, the easier it becomes for the next generation, and the easier it becomes for you. If there's one of you, it's a token, but if there's three, you start creating the norm around the table.

Becoming inspired, knowing yourself and celebrating strengths are the three cornerstones of the work we do to raise our confidence in ourselves and our capabilities. Building confidence is a process and not a switch. We have to keep stretching our confidence-building muscle for it to continue working.

The Female Leads we interviewed over the past five years also have seven key commonalities that have helped them step into the room and remain there. We will cover all of these in Chapter 5, beginning with feeding our passions.

SEVEN WISDOMS OF FEMALE LEADS

How does someone become a Female Lead? This is a question we have been asking ourselves since the beginning. To try and answer it, we have interviewed nearly 300 women who have excelled in diverse arenas. These women have influenced and led their communities, often pushing into the macro areas of economic or decision-making power. From these interviews, we noticed seven common threads of the advice they offer to other women who want to follow in their footsteps. These are:

1. Feed your passions
2. Stay curious
3. Ask for help
4. Dare to be different
5. Find strength in setbacks
6. Accept self-doubt
7. Own your accomplishments

These commonalities have helped women to step forward and be present in the room. We believe these fundamental truths are crucial for shaping the next generation of female leaders but can also inspire women of any age.

1. FEED YOUR PASSIONS

I have met Julie Bentley many times, and on each occasion she is utterly engaging. She was passionate about her work as Chief Executive of Girl Guiding UK and is a true grassroots campaigner. When we interviewed her for our first book, *The Female Lead: Women Who Shape Our World*, she explained that she had actively decided to commit to a career in the not-for-profit sector. She reasoned that we spend most of our life at work and therefore need to know we're doing something worthwhile. As she said:

> We're put on the earth for a certain period of time and we have a choice how to use it. I want to make the most positive contribution I can, and I believe that working with young people is a good way of doing that, because they are the future.

Having authentic passions and interests, and pursuing them, can transform someone's life. Being passionate is about having a deep and lasting belief, as Julie's is about making a positive contribution to young people's lives, and is rarely just about making money or seeking fame. When we are passionate about something, it is inevitably propelled by our super strengths and can grow if we invest in it, through hard work and a disciplined focus. Our natural talents are gifts, but our passion and ambition require real commitment, as dreams rarely come true without bumps and bruises along the way. We need to show creativity, dedication and resilience. We must also be true to ourselves and realistic. For example, we can't all become supermodels even if we want to be.

When we are passionate about something, there is a commitment to it and investment in our learning and growth. We are honing and strengthening this skill all the time. We can feel strongly about something and have an interest in it, but this is different from a sense of purpose that consumes us. It is a roller-coaster ride of times when everything seems to go wrong through to the biggest highs when it all comes together brilliantly, and we feel fulfilled and exhilarated. It can be challenging and exhausting, but we never stop loving it. It never leaves us. It might go dormant for a while, but we return to it consistently because there is a thread inside us that pulls us back. We do it because something tells us that this is what we are meant to do. It's a driving force beyond financial rewards or public recognition.

Discovering our passion cannot be rushed or forced, and sometimes it finds us. Women speak about the moment they responded instinctively to an injustice or a need they felt compelled to solve or became committed to helping with. Feeding our passions is about first discovering them by trying out different things until something produces a deep calling in us. This ties in with becoming inspired, where we give ourselves the time and stimulus to explore what qualities we admire in others, what we are drawn to in history or in others we meet. The second part is allowing ourselves to explore our passions fully without seeing them as a waste of time or something for our younger or older self. If we are lucky, our purpose in life can be whatever we choose to make it. It is ours to discover and not for others to decide. But often, we don't identify the genuine driver that makes us who we are and instead focus on pleasing others by trying to have the life and career *they* think we should.

Our passions are very much linked to fulfilment. Once we discover and cultivate them, they will remain with us for a lifetime. If we are lucky enough to find work involving one or more of them, it will transform our working life into something truly gratifying.

One of my passions is understanding people. Not in a way that relates to psychotherapy but in a way which reveals distinct patterns about people, both their differences and similarities. It's a science I became addicted to because I learned the essential skills early on and trained my brain to think in this way. I found that the more I practised, the easier and more rewarding it became. This passion for understanding people united my husband and me and bound together two polar opposite personalities and skills.

I am also passionate about building something of substance and value that can be applied at scale. Through The Female Lead, I sincerely believe in showing men and women that women are not all the same. For example, a company cannot change its maternity package and think it has ticked the box for 'dealt with women's requirements' for the next 10 years. Women want and need different support at different stages in their life. Our age and lifestyle change our focus. However, within that vast breadth of half the world's population, there are uniting factors that we should seek out and these can be provided through data.

2. STAY CURIOUS

As a Pulitzer Prize-winning author and former US Ambassador to the United Nations, it is not surprising that Samantha Power is curious about the world. She has had a fascinating and varied career that she attributes to following her gut. She moved to the Balkans without a job and ended up as a war reporter. She later left law school to work on a book because the topic had seized her. None of these steps were made on a conventional path, but the career rewards have been huge. When we interviewed her, she told us her advice for young people would be not to decide on a title and try to script a path towards it. Instead, they should develop their interests and dig into them – go deep instead of wide.

All of the Female Leads we have interviewed are driven by a curiosity about the world – they are hungry to expand their horizons and learn new things, even if they don't apply this knowledge directly to their jobs or studies. This is because they see value in learning. This rounded view takes them in new directions and expands their creativity. It can also enhance their work as they can view it from different angles and it ultimately contributes to their success and sense of purpose and fulfilment.

For me, staying curious is the most important of the seven. I love the energy I get from learning and how it informs me on a personal and professional level. Curiosity keeps us growing and in a youthful state of mind as we learn about and respect what goes on in the world around us. In my opinion, there is nothing worse than a pompous old person who thinks that they know it all and looks down on others with disdain. They are the embodiment of a closed mind that doesn't think they have any more to learn from anyone else. They also open themselves up to being proven wrong. I remember telling a very senior leader, who was well respected in his industry, what I did and my vision for my work. He laughed at my explanation and said that data would never be strategic. How wrong he was.

Staying curious is about knowing that you have never finished with your learning, whatever your age. There is always more to find out, more to be taught and more that you can be. It is about listening, learning, striving and being focused on personal growth.

3. ASK FOR HELP

Asking for help ties in well with staying curious. If we are curious about the world and know there will be some limitations to our understanding or skills, at some point we will be faced with two choices. The first is that we remain where we are. The second is that we move forward by expanding our knowledge or collaborating with others.

Asking for help can often wrongly be perceived as a sign of weakness, an indication of where we are lacking, when in reality it is the opposite. Self-knowledge is incredibly powerful, and if we know the areas where we need help and seek a solution, we grow as people. It also shows that we respect the skills of others and encourages collaboration.

As Christine Lagarde, the President of the European Central Bank and Managing Director of the International Monetary Fund from 2011 to 2019, wisely told us:

> Helping others, being helped, operating with others on your team is critically important. Some people will not be helpful and some people will want to promote themselves instead of the group. But that is not a reason to assume that you can succeed on your own.

She also encouraged us to reach out to other women, including more senior women who have succeeded, and ask them for advice and support, which I believe is key when it comes to asking for help.

4. DARE TO BE DIFFERENT

Many of the Female Leads have revealed how different they felt from their peers in form, style or approach when they were younger, but they embraced these differences and turned them to their advantage. Standing out might feel uncomfortable at the time, but it can set us apart and get us noticed.

Often, when we are young, we feel an overwhelming pressure to fit in with our peers and try desperately to become invisible. The wisdom among the Female Leads is that even at a young age, we should resist this urge and instead embrace what makes us different. The ballerina, Michaela DePrince, phrased it beautifully: 'Don't be afraid to be a poppy in a field of daffodils.'

When we dare to be different, we do this to be true to our authentic selves. We break the mould of what is expected of us and don't conform to archetypes. As the author and editor, Tina Brown, explains about her own experience as a teenager:

> I was a rebel and I was expelled from three boarding schools. That kind of subversiveness is useful – you should always question everything and push boundaries. I regard getting slung out of those schools as a badge of pride because they were such uptight, upscale boarding schools that any budding journalist would want to rebel.

5. FIND STRENGTH IN SETBACKS

When Liv Cooke qualified for the Freestyle Football World Championships in Melbourne, she knew she was still the new kid on the block. But she also knew she deserved to be there. Liv told us that she had devoted herself to her dream and even quit college. A few days before the competition, she injured her foot but decided to compete anyway. In the final, that small injury went from a stress fracture to a full fracture. She had just been ranked second in the world, but her career was now hanging in the balance. It didn't stop her though. She made a clear decision that she was going back for gold, even if it meant being out of action for five months. She knew she had what it took, and the following year she proved it by becoming the Freestyle Football World Champion.

Whatever path we are on, there will be times when things don't work out the way we imagined they would. This is to be expected as there are many factors that we don't have control over or can anticipate. However, the Female Leads viewed setbacks as a chance to learn, and this is how they found strength in them.

In my experience, we learn far more when things go wrong than when they go to plan. This is because we often don't know why something went right, and this makes it difficult to extract the key ingredient we should replicate next time as we can rarely replicate the entire situation each time.

In the business world, this can extend to not knowing why people agreed to work with you or your company. You will only find out how your business is viewed by potential customers when they decide *not* to work with you and provide feedback on what influenced their decision. This can have a huge impact because you might wrongly imagine that clients work with you because you are a low-cost solution, when in reality, they might be working with you because of your past experience and consider your prices to be very reasonable for a guaranteed outcome. However, if a client decides not to work with you, they might explain the reasoning behind their decision is that they don't feel confident that you can deliver. This means you don't have to squeeze down your prices, and can also focus on ensuring delivery and conveying how you do this to the next potential client.

Setbacks can teach us how to problem-solve, which is an enormously important skill. We will all reach a point where we have taken a wrong turn, or something isn't working as expected. The question is, how do we work around it? We might take a different route, ask a different person for their input or advice or present an idea in a better way. Problem-solving can often be the most exhausting part of creativity as we are trying to anticipate an outcome that can never be guaranteed. But, if we think about it, we are problem-solving every day, just on a smaller scale, so we rarely notice it. For example, figuring out how we can get our work done, do the food shopping and pick up our children on time. Problem-solving is like exercising a muscle, and the more we practise it, the easier it gets.

Lastly, setbacks can also be very motivational, particularly if they involve being underestimated or ignored, as these can trigger feelings of anger and injustice. These emotions can drive us to try harder and succeed the next time.

6. ACCEPT SELF-DOUBT

The vast majority of Female Leads we have spoken with have admitted to experiencing imposter syndrome or feelings of self-doubt. They have accepted this as an inevitable feature of aiming high. It was not a barrier to achievement but a reminder that success and stature are not entitlements. Learning to live with these feelings and overcoming them is the key to returning to a passion and not giving up on it. As Lady Brenda Hale, President of the Supreme Court from 2017 to 2020, put it:

> I defy anybody not to have had imposter syndrome and be any good at what they do. When I first went to the high school, the only girl from my little village school, I thought, *What am I doing here?* When I went to Cambridge, I pinched myself and thought, *I am so pleased to be here, but is it me?* When I went to the Law Commission – the first woman, and surrounded by very confident, intellectually impressive people – I thought, *Can I really do it?*

I honestly believe that every successful entrepreneur (who isn't a complete narcissist) has experienced self-doubt because it is a natural response to a challenging situation. At The Female Lead, our data shows that self-confidence is something women struggle with the most. No one is utterly self-confident, and if they come across that way, they are usually just pretending to be. To overcome this perception that others have confidence and we do not, we need to normalise self-doubt and not view it as a weakness within ourselves. Self-doubt is a sign that we are reaching further than before and trying to do our very best. To do that, we need to feel the fear, embrace it and try again, even if we fail the first few times. We can always assess where we might need help. This is a way of searching for a better answer or solution and is a sign of intelligence and bravery. This restlessness to do better is what sets a successful entrepreneur apart. What protects them and keeps them going is the belief that they will ultimately find a way through.

Self-doubt is lifelong in a journey of continuous improvement. Are you doing enough? Are you doing it the right way? Are you making a difference? What is the personal cost? The collective wisdom around self-doubt or imposter syndrome is to embrace it, use it to be more conscientious, and work harder where needed. It also encourages curiosity when you want to check whether you have missed or forgotten something. Constant doubt about your path is healthy but give yourself credit that you have what it takes to get there in the end.

When we embrace the benefits of self-doubt, when we push outside of our comfort zone, we can become better at what we do. However, one of the times that we have to tackle self-doubt head-on and lessen its hold is if it interferes with our sleep, as lack of sleep genuinely slows us down and weakens our ability to prob-lem-solve. In these situations, we have to be kind to ourselves the next day, recognise that we're just having a bad day and not cata-strophise that this means a bad life or a bad career, or that it is a sign of what is to come.

Another area where women commonly have self-doubt that can be overcome is worrying over whether they have said the wrong thing or acted inappropriately. Too much time can be spent anxiously imagining how something was interpreted or if they hurt or misled someone unintentionally. This type of self-doubt can raise anxiety levels disproportionately, shift our focus onto past events that we can't change and wastes our precious mental energy. If you said something with good intentions at the time, try to move on from it and don't agonise about it. This anxious reflec-tion doesn't seem to be something that men struggle with as much, which might be because women are more likely to be condi-tioned to be people-pleasers. This fear of people not liking us often prevents us from taking the bold, brilliant steps we need to reach our full potential and signals that we might not yet have found the right supportive community. It is easier and perhaps wiser to aim for others to respect (or even admire) us rather than seeking 'likes'.

7. OWN YOUR ACCOMPLISHMENTS

The final commonality among the Female Leads is that they are able to give themselves credit for their achievements rather than passing them off as luck or diminishing their hard work. For so long, women have been conditioned to be modest, and we have internalised this, becoming overly concerned with not appearing as though we are boasting. This reluctance to own our accomplishments can cause us to fear success more than failure. Fear of rejection or negative feedback from others can create insidious damage that holds us back in all areas of our lives, including promotion, and asking for pay rises or flexibility.

I'll always remember speaking with Anne-Marie Imafidon and her outlining her education and the way she is still perceived to this day. She told me:

> I did two GCSEs aged 10: one in Maths and one in ICT. Aged 11, I did my computing A level, and I did an AS in Maths, and I went up to study at Oxford aged 17. I'd finished my master's by the time I was 20. In terms of being underestimated, this is something I'm encountering much more as an adult than I did as a child. I'm always the youngest, the blackest, the female-est person, whether it's in board meetings, in pitch scenarios, in media, in certain rooms. For me, it's always a funny one, almost, to kind of play the underdog, and arrive at the event and be treated a particular way –

and then watch the shock on the faces when I stand up and I am the keynote, part of the reason why they turned up.

For many women, an inclination to play down our achievements can be overwhelming and becomes an automatic reflex. It forms part of the belief in being polite and not big-headed. 'Oh, that, it was nothing. It wasn't difficult. I had lots of help. I got lucky.' These are all things we say automatically, and the outcome is that they minimise our work and contribution. I learned from personal experience that if we make less of our accomplishments, we risk diminishing the efforts of our team and those looking to us for leadership and positive encouragement.

Tips: Owning our accomplishments

- When we are complimented, we often respond by either dismissing our accomplishments – 'I got lucky' – or by attacking them – 'It doesn't look as good as I had wanted'.
- This desire to downplay our achievements often stems from a need to be liked, which is many women's Achilles heel.
- If we want to reach the top of any profession, we will need to discard the need to be liked by everyone. If we aim to be liked by everyone, we will fail because we cannot please everyone, no matter what we do, and we will pull back from making bold decisions.
- Wanting to be liked doesn't always come across as likeable. It can also come across as weak or insincere or that we are just a 'yes' person.

- Aim to be respected rather than liked.
- Simply saying 'thank you' when someone compliments you or your work acknowledges their interest in you without you explaining away your successes.

Adept communicators will tell you that what they've done is important. They don't explain the minutiae or the process of reaching the final product or discovery. Instead, they will say, 'This is huge', 'This will impact your life or business', or 'It's never been done before'. For an audience to recognise the importance of your work, you have to let them know that what you did was hard or special. This ties into daring to be different because we are making sure that we stand out by acknowledging that our accomplishment is important.

*   *   *

These seven commonalities are how Female Leads strive and thrive through the myriad of situations life can throw at us.

The next stage we work on is what is balanced in our life right now and what is not. These are the Six Pillars of Fulfilment. We explore the informative data and inspiring stories for each one, and how we can use them to push beyond the boundaries of the self and into our communities.

PART II

EMPOWERING WOMEN THROUGH FULFILMENT

CHAPTER 6

THE SIX PILLARS OF FULFILMENT

What is fulfilment, and why is it so important to us? Fulfilment is when we have already satisfied our basic needs, such as food and shelter, and have the ability to strive to become the best versions of ourselves and all that we can possibly be.

Fulfilment is the key to self-confidence. If we feel that what we do has meaning, whatever arena that might be in, our actions are purposeful, and we know that what we do matters, and it builds our confidence. With strengthening self-confidence, we are more likely to understand and head for what will make us feel fulfilled because we will be doing what we are passionate about. Fulfilment and self-confidence therefore feed into and encourage each other.

Fulfilment requires self-awareness. You will need to know the balance of priorities you require and want at your stage of life. It is also about understanding what drives you, your passions, skills and super strengths – it is an awareness of what makes you special.

If we don't know in which area of our life we require fulfilment, there will usually be a feeling of something missing or that we are not quite on the right path. There will be an absence of purpose, and if we are not careful, we can spend a lifetime trying to work out what it is. Conversely, if we are aware of where we find fulfilment, we can protect and expand on what satisfies us the most and know when to repair what is satisfying us the least.

The Female Lead has simplified this process by creating a survey that looks at three key areas that create a fulfilled life. These are:

1. Emotional elements: How you feel when completely fulfilled, such as calm or confident.
2. Functional elements: The importance you place on things like work, relationships and money.
3. Lifestyle factors: A detailed look into each area of your lifestyle, such as relationships or work life.

We have used these three key areas to categorise all the potential areas of fulfilment into six lifestyle pillars that affect women's overall fulfilment. If you decided to take the persona test (see Chapter 3), then you will already be aware of what areas of fulfilment are important to you, and where you are the most and least fulfilled. You will have a primary and secondary area of fulfilment based on which persona you are (that everyone with the same persona will share), but the results on how fulfilled you are in these areas will be unique to you and based on your responses.

The Six Pillars of Fulfilment are:

1. Self
2. Health
3. Relationships
4. Work
5. Money
6. Society

We chose these six pillars by looking at our social-media following of nearly 8 million people. We used the six conversation topics we received the most engagement about to choose the pillars because these were the conversations that women wanted to have (see Figure 6.1). By using global research over time, we wanted to understand how women make trade-offs between these key pillars. As well as exploring the average scores of each pillar, we also wanted to see how often a pillar is the most important to an individual. For some people who take our survey, there will be joint first place and these are counted towards both pillars.

There is a very clear hierarchy across the six pillars in terms of importance. Women's clear prime concern is Relationships. As we will explore in Chapter 8, these are not just intimate relationships but also friendships, and relationships with family, people at work and our children. The second most important area to women is Self, followed by Health, Work, Money and Society. However, these average scores hide a high degree of variability both by age and country.

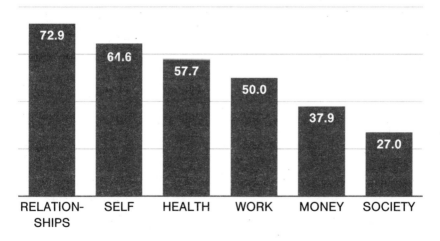

Figure 6.1 Overall importance of Six Pillars of Fulfilment.

We managed to gather enough data from twelve countries to be able to explore women's responses on a geographic basis as well. The majority of our replies are from the UK and USA, but we also have sufficient data from Ireland, France, Germany, the Netherlands, Switzerland and Sweden in Europe, as well as from Australia, New Zealand, Canada and India.

What is really interesting is that geographically we see several quite distinctive patterns that show that where a respondent lives can shape what is important to them, and how these priorities can sometimes cross borders in an increasingly globalised world. The United Kingdom and Ireland have very similar patterns on all measures, and these are quite similar to Australia and New Zealand as well. The United States and Canada are alike, but Canada shows a stronger alignment with Australia rather than the USA. All of these dominantly English-speaking nations show related patterns, with very strong scores for Relationships and lower than average scores for Self. The main exception is that the USA stands slightly apart with a weaker score on Relationships and a stronger score on Money.

Germany, Sweden, the Netherlands and Switzerland also form a natural grouping, although there are a few interesting differences, primarily in responses to the Work and Relationships pillars. France is an outlier to its European neighbours, with much higher scores for Self and Health. Finally, India is very distinctive, with Money, Work and Self being much higher than other countries, which probably reflects their economic realities compared to the other countries we gathered data on.

There is one key difference between the personas and the pillars that we all need to be aware of. The personas reflect the emotions we experience when we are fulfilled. Whereas the pillars are clear areas of our life that we can take control of. It is difficult to consciously change persona, although they usually change throughout your lifetime as you age. But once you are aware of the things within each pillar that lead to you being satisfied or dissatisfied with this area of your life, you can turn your attention to them and increase the fulfilment you find.

*   *   *

These pillars of fulfilment and personas are not unique to women as the science we use also applies to men. Many men will have the same pillars of fulfilment, although they may weight some of them differently. Men can (and do) take the personas and pillars surveys and anecdotally we have been told that even though the results use the pronouns 'she' and 'her', men still find they reflect their personalities.

Up until now, there hasn't been much mention of men in this book, but this is not because I believe they are the problem and should be scrubbed from these pages. The aim is never to lay this inequality at their feet and say they are responsible. How we got here is far more layered and nuanced than that. Conversations about inequality have to happen, and for men to hear them they can't take place away from male communities. Something that is missing from feminism is that it appears to alienate men, either intentionally or unintentionally. There is often an effort to involve men, but they're rarely present at the events that I attend. There is a real danger that we're having meetings among ourselves and agreeing furiously with each other without changing a single thing.

Men have to be part of this conversation because it is not an 'us versus them' scenario – they can also be our allies. This is because if women are excluded from a workplace that was designed by men, men feel trapped by it. The workplace is an old construct that doesn't serve the needs of most members of modern society and therefore there is a reduction in the fulfilment it provides. When we realise that the pillars of fulfilment apply to both men and women, it is a unifying force.

Often the data we are shown, including data on health and work, is based on evidence collected from men. At The Female Lead, we have gathered data from women, but we can also apply this wisdom to men as we believe it is relevant to all. The data shows women's priorities within the pillars at different times of their lives and in relation to their personal circumstances. We also include the stories we have collected for each pillar to bring some life and vibrancy to them, not as a ground truth. These provide inspiration, reassure women that they are not alone in what they are facing and provide a community of millions.

Like our personas, where we find fulfilment shifts throughout our lifetime, this is fundamental to our understanding because it shows, yet again, that women are not one large homogeneous group. What a 20-year-old finds fulfilling is not necessarily the same for a 40-year-old. It is about knowing the balance between our areas of fulfilment and how important it is to us that our priorities are met in particular areas. How much money is enough? How much work do I want, and how will it fit in with my other responsibilities? How much do I need to think about my health?

When women are empowered in the areas that are important to them, they can then begin transmitting this to their communities, bringing about any further change needed within them. When women are empowered in the areas that are important to them, they can then begin transmitting this to their communities, bringing about any further change needed within them – and the results of our LinkedIn poll show that this is what they are interested in. Finally, when women's needs are met on this level, their ability to expand into the areas of decision-makers and economic influence on the macro level increases, which we will cover in Part III.

In a recent poll on LinkedIn, we asked our audience, 'What topic would you be most interested in learning about?' We received 26,208 votes and the responses were:

- How to influence and make an impact: 46%
- Navigating career and motherhood: 21%
- Effective communication: 21%
- What makes a good leader: 12%

As Nit Ambani, Chair and Founder of the Reliance Foundation, confirmed to us:

When women have goals and aspirations, they positively impact their families and communities. Through our work at the Reliance Foundation, we have seen that every time a woman does well for herself, she has the power to open opportunities for other women too.

Before we reach the macro level, let's take a brief look at the six pillars and some of the Female Leads who epitomise them, before exploring them fully in the following chapters:

SELF

When Hannah Graf came to one of our photoshoots, she made a wonderful impact. After we had captured a photograph that was both a relaxed but powerful pose she told her story to us.

I grew up in Cardiff with my mum, my dad and older brother. As early as I can remember, I was questioning my gender. I'd never heard the word 'transgender'. All I knew was that I didn't click with the body that I had or the role in society that people expected me to play. I spent a lot of my childhood and teenage years feeling unsettled and uneasy, and that I was the only person like me in the world.

I was in the Army Cadets and an instructor said, 'You could do this for a job.' That piqued my interest and I applied to a military college where you did A levels and military activities. Then I went to Newcastle University and got an Engineering degree, before heading to the Royal Military Academy Sandhurst to become an officer.

There is a school of thought that, before we come out, transgender women choose hypermasculine roles in order to prove to ourselves, and the wider world, that we are the men society says we are. That is partially true, but equally, I loved physical activity, being outdoors, the teamwork and camaraderie. I find it strange that people think that women – trans or otherwise – shouldn't be in the army when there is nothing about those qualities that is inherently unfeminine.

Being a closeted trans person is a strange experience. On the outside I was happy: I'd been to Sandhurst, I'd become an officer and was in a leadership role. Everything seemed positive but I was living this hidden life. Everything came to a head on a tour of duty in Afghanistan. It's a place where there is no time off, you are working seven days a week and have no private space. I lived in a tent with seven guys and there was no internet access, no TV. It led to a large amount of introspection and I realised that, if I didn't do something, I was going to live an unhappy and unfulfilled life.

Hannah's passion around fulfilment speaks to the very heart of what I am trying to do with The Female Lead campaign.

*　*　*

When we talk about 'Self' as a pillar, it means how we feel about ourselves and take care of ourselves. Women have to live with so many competing expectations from the world around them. They are expected to look perfect, have successful careers, be mothers, get married (and live happily ever after) and be strong but also nurturing. Building self-worth is complex when there is so much pressure to meet all of these standards of what it means to be a woman today. Part of this process is that we have to learn to tune out what others expect of us and instead prioritise our own needs, or at least put them as equal to others in our lives, and give ourselves the care and reflection we all deserve. Self encompasses:

- Confidence
- Resilience
- Looking and feeling good
- Mental wellbeing
- Impact at work

- Role in relationships
- Contribution to society

RELATIONSHIPS

When we interviewed the multi-Grammy-winning singer Sheryl Crow, she told us that her view on her relationships changed when she became sick with breast cancer. At that point she decided to examine her self-appointed role of being a caretaker and a people-pleaser. It was a real turning point in learning how to put herself first and to say no, at the risk of people not being happy with her. She found it very liberating. Two of the most beautiful things that came out of it were her two adopted boys. Sheryl explained that although she came to motherhood as an older mum, she felt that by the time her boys arrived, she had done everything she wanted to. She saw it as a gift that all of her attention could go to the very thing that brought her the most joy.

We know from our own research into women's fulfilment that, broadly speaking, they value their relationships with partners, friends, family and colleagues above everything in life. This may be innate or due to social conditioning. For centuries women have been taught to be nurturing and responsible for the emotional wellbeing of others. At the same time, women still carry the unequal burden of household and care responsibilities across the world. This contributes not only to the gender pay gap, but is also a likely source of distress, making depression more common in women worldwide. Therefore there are two sides to certain types of relationships: the amount of importance we place on them, and the expectations placed on us to care for others. Relationships encompasses relationships with:

- Partner
- Parents
- Friends
- Colleagues
- Children
- Boss

HEALTH

Health is a pillar often not thought of when we have good health, but once that is taken away, it becomes much more important. Our focus on our health also grows steadily as we age. The topics within health also change with our life stages, such as focusing on fertility in our younger years and on preventative screening in our older ones. When we talk about 'health', we are not just discussing female health such as periods, childbirth and menopause. As well as all aspects of our physical health, it also incorporates our mental health and the physical and mental health of those around us. Health encompasses:

- Physical health
- Female health, such as fertility and menopause
- Family health
- Preventative health
- Holistic
- Mental health

As we age, our health naturally becomes of more concern to us, yet so much research into common conditions is still needed. As the neurobiologist Dr Cori Bargmann explained to us for our first book, *The Female Lead: Women Who Shape Our World*:

> I feel that, in our era, the brain is the focus for exciting exploration of the unknown, in the way that the moon was in the 1960s. I am one of the people who helped plan the BRAIN initiative. On a small scale, in my own lab, I hope we might have something useful to say about mental health, about depression and the way that emotional and motivational states make the brain function in different ways. On a large scale, through the BRAIN initiative, my role is to help thousands of scientists in different places to do something for brain disorders. They say one person in three – that's one member of your family – will have some sort of serious disorder affecting the brain during his or her life, whether it's Alzheimer's, Parkinson's, depression, schizophrenia or autism, so the medical need is tremendous.

WORK

The gender pay gap is still pronounced and far from closing. Women still have this loss of earnings primarily because of the multiple roles they have to balance in their households. The workplaces we operate in were designed decades ago and do not consider the requirements of our family lives as well. Many women have welcomed the introduction of hybrid working, but this also holds hidden risks to women's careers. Both men and women will benefit from working conditions that reflect the altered world that we live in. Not only will this make women's working lives more rewarding and fulfilling, but it will also stimulate economic growth for everyone through true equality at work. Work encompasses:

- The gender pay gap
- Promotion and career development
- Fair pay
- Flexible working
- Maternity and childcare support
- Leadership support
- Mentor support

A business leader who I have met many times at key panels and admire for the energy she invests in stimulating healthy debate is Vanessa Kingori OBE, the Publishing Director of British *Vogue*. When we interviewed her for The Female Lead, she told us that she was working with the Royal College of Obstetricians and Gynaecologists on the maternal process and that topics such as endometriosis and fibroids often came up. She went on to explain that:

There is so little funding and research, and such little consideration for how these things impact a woman's life, work and wider health. Many women also feel talking openly about these issues puts us at a disadvantage at work. For women to have an equal footing with men, we need some different considerations, so need the space to bring our whole selves to our roles, whether in the home or at work. A lot of the things that we've been taught to hide away and 'push through' are just part of who we are. We need to stop hiding the female experience in order to level the playing field and get the best from women.

MONEY

There is no greater protection for a woman than money of her own. It is integral to our freedom and equality, yet women tend not to talk about money. Discussing money has long been seen as unfeminine, impolite or dull, but the silence is detrimental. Although, globally, women still earn less and have smaller savings and pensions than men, there is progress, and women are talking more openly about finances than they did even 20 years ago. These conversations need to continue if we are going to see a significant closing of the gender money gap. Money encompasses:

- Personal finances
- Pensions
- The money gap
- Unpaid work

Gina Miller, an entrepreneur and social justice campaigner, is a formidable and brilliant role model. I have shared speaker platforms with her several times and as a former lawyer her arguments are always well-framed. She is also eloquent and unforgiving whenever she finds inequality and unfairness. One of the topics she spoke with us about is women's relationship with money. She said:

I discovered that I was quite good at business, and coming up with ideas, and marketing, and being an entrepreneur, so that's what I went into. Regaining my sense of control was very attractive. And my early discovery that money gives you freedom drew me to financial services.

I'm very passionate for women to discover that real freedom requires you to be in control of your financial health. As a country, we talk about a pay gap, but the pension gap is even more of a concern. Women have a bad relationship with money because that's the way society is constructed. Through the centuries, women have been told it is not their place to be in the workplace, to be in control of money. That's a social construct we still have a long way to go to dismantle. There is nothing shameful about being ambitious or wanting to earn a good wage or wanting to be in a position where you can use your money to help others, to help society and to make a difference. Money is power and women should have access to that power.

SOCIETY

Gender inequality has real consequences for society as a whole and for every individual. Violence against women, objectification and discrimination are a danger to women's lives and to their mental and physical health. Across the world, the subtle day-to-day forms of sexism can impact a woman's sense of wellbeing and success negatively. This bias is even more oppressive when we consider intersectionality in the forms of race, disability, sexual orientation and religion.

We know that inequality not only affects the lives of individuals but also stunts economic growth and hinders development. Women bear the brunt of poverty, and their empowerment is central to its elimination. The Society pillar includes:

- Gender equality
- Female representation
- Ethnic discrimination
- Social equality
- Environment
- Social media

The activist and founder of the Me Too movement, Tarana Burke, told us about her approach to activism for our second book, *The Female Lead (Volume II): We Rise By Lifting Others*. She explained that:

Our response to sexual violence should look like our response to gun violence or police violence. We should be organising, we should be coming together to understand the roots of the problem, we should be looking at prevention and healing. I'd spent most of my life feeling like I was a particular kind of girl and that's why these things happened to me, so I was steeped in shame. As soon as I connected to others who understood deeply what I had experienced, whether they were survivors or just had the ability to empathise, the layers of shame started to peel away. I knew that there was power in empathy and that whatever work I did had to be driven by that. The idea of empowerment through empathy came before the name 'Me Too' because empathy is what changed my life.

We need to take steps to disrupt rape culture, which creates the space for violence to happen. The steps are tangible: in America 20 years ago, we smoked cigarettes everywhere and that's not the case now. It took multiple interventions: we had community intervention where people organised to get cigarette machines out of schools and public areas, and medical intervention with research about what tobacco does to your body and the dangers of second-hand smoke. It took years of organising and strategising to get to the point where, when a person pulls out a cigarette, we're like, 'Ooh, you're trying to kill us!'

The same can happen with sexual violence if we collectively decide to intervene. We need cultural, political, medical and narrative interventions and we all need to work in tandem. That's why we created an addendum to 'Me Too' called 'Act Too', because everybody has a role to play. If we stopped showing egregious sexual violence on television and in movies that would be a massive shift. We need research initiatives showing the cost of sexual violence – the money lost in wages and medical bills; the long-term effects of PTSD on a person. Comprehensive sex education is also needed.

These pillars of fulfilment show that not all women are the same. Therefore there is no one-size-fits-all solution either. Instead, there are strong indicators of what women need at different stages of their lives and depending on their circumstances. Of course it is always much easier to highlight the problems surrounding inequality rather than focusing on solutions, but without solutions, we are just talking about the problem and not making any progress.

Therefore, the solutions come from acknowledging the pillars in life that are most important to women at different stages and supporting them through either their self-development or from a government, business or school perspective. By bringing all of this data together into one place, it is only then that we can start looking collectively at how to make any significant changes.

We begin this process with the Self pillar, which is about how we view and feel about ourselves, including our confidence, resilience and mental health.

CHAPTER 7

SELF

When we wrote our second book, *The Female Lead* (Volume II): *We Rise By Lifting Others*, we asked all of the Female Leads we featured to bring an important object with them and tell us about it. I will always remember Megan Crabbe, a pioneer in the body positivity movement, telling us about what she had brought with her. It was a letter her dad had given her when she was 18 years old. He wrote that it didn't matter to him what she did professionally, where she chose to live or who she chose to love; he would always be proud of her as long as she acted with integrity. To him, that meant being true to her values and standing up for what she believed in. Megan told us that she always tries to hold onto those words when she's unsure why she is doing something or if she's facing a decision. It is that integrity of being true to ourselves which is so important to the notion of 'Self'.

We begin with the Self pillar because it leads naturally from the first part of the book, which was all about discovering who we are, what we want, the area of our strengths, what drives us, and who we can join and form a community with. We also find that the Self pillar is the area that most people who take our survey choose to explore first about themselves.

The Self pillar encompasses and continues this self-discovery – how we feel about ourselves, our self-care, the expectations that are placed on us, our own needs and our sense of self. It includes our self-esteem, but also our role in the world. Self is about our identity, which is vitally important, and what we hope for and believe in. As the actress May Calamawy said to us for an article we wrote with her, 'I really think what I hope is more women can grow up learning to trust themselves and their intuition. And just follow that, regardless. If I listened to everyone, I wouldn't be here.'

When we talk about the Self pillar it encompasses:

- Confidence and self-belief
- Resilience
- Looking and feeling good inside and out
- Mental wellbeing
- Impact in life and at work
- Role in relationships and family
- Contribution and role in society

Confidence, on the whole, is not easily seen or assumed by women, and our society is more encouraging towards men. As singer-songwriter Joy Crookes explains it:

Society doesn't naturally favour women and my experience in the music industry is that I have sometimes had to be loud for people to hear my voice. And that takes confidence, and self-assurance and self-belief to make that noise and be heard. Imposter syndrome is inevitable for anyone who works with the public. I don't ignore it, I acknowledge it: okay, you're there, but I still need to write these songs and get on this stage. I think that learning to live with the voice in my head has actually made it quieter.

Society expects women to work hard, be good at their job and care for their families. Of equal emphasis, they are also expected to be polite, respectful and well turned out. So much of women's confidence is wrapped up in how they look. This is because girls are fed different messages from boys as they grow up. As the chef, Asma Khan, said when we interviewed her:

The fear of losing, of being laughed at and ridiculed by others, holds so many of us back. When people told me, 'You are so overweight that no one will ever marry you', or said, 'You are not graceful, you're not the kind of girl that our family is proud of', it did hit me – I did feel bad. I would tell myself, 'Pick yourself up.' You are more than your dress size, your bank balance, your Instagram followers, the car you drive. You are more than that. I would tell my teenage self: 'One day, the world will know your name.'

From a young age, the media emphasises that how women look is incredibly important to the impact they make in the workplace. If you don't feel you have reached these standards, you can quickly lose confidence. We observe that many women invest hours every day in honing and perfecting their looks. They often follow celebrities and fashion on both social and traditional media. They invest energy in seeking perfection, but often experience opposition and a lack of support because of the workplace's traditional male constructs and reward schemes.

I've always tried to build my sense of confidence by what I do rather than how I look, as it's an easier journey to focus on and infinitely more pleasurable. You can be in control of what you do, but you cannot always be in control of how you look. We're all dealt a shuffled hand of genes when we're born, and some things can't be altered. Even though I've always been aware of this, there have been times in my life when I have felt uncomfortable about my looks. After my first child, I felt out of shape. My suits didn't fit anymore, but I still had to get dressed and step back into those challenging boardrooms. I felt vulnerable in a way I hadn't experienced before. My body was programmed to care for a newborn. Instead, I was asking it to tackle tough conversations in tight suits with new bulges and when not feeling anywhere near as groomed as I used to. I'm not sure that anyone really, truly, doesn't care how they look – even if it's just a little. The secret to sanity and a balanced life seems to be not caring too much because self-critical thoughts can make you spiral. I felt so lucky to love my job but also have the gift of children. I decided I was lucky and I needed to be kind to my poor over-worked body. I might have looked a bit frazzled for a few years, but people just had to put up with it.

When we interviewed her, the make-up artist and entrepreneur Bobbi Brown told us that the mantra that inspired her approach to make-up was: Looking like yourself was what's most beautiful.

The emphasis women put on their looks has been reflected in the data we have gathered. It is also incredibly insightful when it comes to how women prioritise and deprioritise their sense of self during different life stages and according to their circumstances. It shows that women place a great deal of importance on their sense of self in their younger years and then this drops significantly when they enter the middle stages of life, particularly for women who have children or who are married. Towards the end of women's lives it then rockets upwards again.

When we see data results like this, it makes me think of what our natural state should be. It would seem that women naturally try to prioritise their sense of self, but once other roles and responsibilities come into play they put others first and shift their priorities away from themselves.

HOW THE IMPORTANCE OF SELF CHANGES AS WE AGE

Even though Self is the most popular pillar for people who take our surveys to explore, overall it comes in as the second priority of the six pillars to women's fulfilment.

Compared to the other pillars the importance of Self varies most dramatically across the life stages. It starts high at age 18-24 but declines rapidly as more responsibilities form. It has its lowest importance in our 40s and 50s, until it can resurge in our later years of 65 and over. This is a clear sign that women put their Self behind them as responsibilities of family, home and work become more significant factors in their lives.

This is confirmed when we look at the importance of the other pillars as women age (see Figure 7.1). Despite the Self pillar being the highest at age 18-24, it is still second to Relationships in importance. It then falls to third place behind Health and Relationships as women age, and remains so in all age groups over 45.

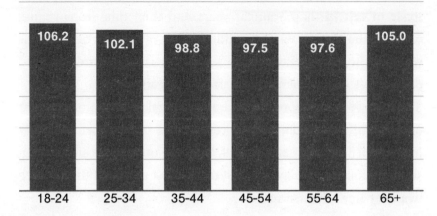

Figure 7.1. Relative importance of Self.

In terms of personas, those most likely to consider the Self pillar most important are the Creator, Reformer and Bon Vivant. Not surprisingly, far fewer Mediators or Influencers rank Self as the most important pillar.

HOW THE IMPORTANCE OF SELF CHANGES DEPENDING ON OUR PERSONAL CIRCUMSTANCES

Overall, the Self pillar is not a priority for women. Regardless of their situation, women find other issues trump Self for most of their life, despite it being the most important area they wish to explore when they participate in our Fulfilment Finder survey (see Chapter 3).

Children make a dramatic difference to the importance of the Self pillar. Women without children are one and a half times more likely to say Self is the most important pillar compared to those with children at home. This dramatic shift in priorities reflects that most women who have children living at home with them are doing it all – they are balancing work, relationships and finances. They therefore put themselves last, and their sense of self is the least important thing to them compared to other aspects of their lives, and compared to other women. Single women rate their sense of self as the second most important pillar, but married women place it nearly last, after all their other needs and wants. It is clear from the data that once women enter long-term relationships or have children they drastically reprioritise their sense of self, losing identity and focus for the sake of others.

Our data also shows the emotions that drive these desires as well. Women with children prioritise feelings of safety and then control, with feelings of excitement and enjoyment taking a back seat while they put their family needs first. In contrast, women without children prioritise excitement and enjoyment, with safety being least important to them.

*　　*　　*

The responses on the Self pillar are a little more volatile than, say, the Relationships pillar, but only vary a little by age and geography. If we look across our measures by country, Self is most important for India and France, and is also highly rated in Germany, the Netherlands, Sweden and Switzerland. It gets the lowest ranking in English-speaking nations, especially the UK and Ireland, followed by the USA, Canada, Australia and New Zealand. However, with the exception of women in France and India, where Self is the top priority, Self is always a second priority to Relationships for the majority of women.

Julia Gillard, 27th Prime Minister of Australia

I'd seen women in politics get on a rollercoaster where they felt better about themselves after a day of good headlines and worse after a day of bad headlines. I'd decided that I wasn't going to do that. I wouldn't let myself be hijacked. I was going to be the same person whatever.

THE TOPICS OF MOST IMPORTANCE WITHIN THE SELF PILLAR BY AGE GROUP

Within the Self pillar there are many sub-topics that are of concern at different stages in women's lives. There are also times when they either feel a large gap in this area of fulfilment or find great satisfaction in it. When we examine the responses between where women feel they are now and where they would like to be, three areas stand out for lack of fulfilment: confidence, mental wellbeing and looking and feeling good. These are closely followed by the impact women have in their work. This reflects much of what I have been trying to address with The Female Lead initiative in ensuring women feel more confident about themselves and the way they can contribute at work.

The women who take our surveys are much happier and more confident in their ability to contribute to society, in their friendships, personal resilience and their role as a mother or partner. The key takeaways for each age group are:

AGE 18-24

- 18–24-year-olds gain most of their fulfilment based on looking and feeling good, followed by their role as a friend.
- They experience a large lack of fulfilment when it comes to their mental wellbeing and their self-confidence.
- They don't feel in control of their sense of self but enjoy the exciting experience of finding out who they are.

AGE 25-34

- When it comes to self, looking and feeling good is very important to most of these women.
- At this stage, their role as a partner or wife begins to have higher levels of importance to their sense of self.
- Many women aged 25–34 experience a gap in emotional satisfaction when it comes to feelings of excitement and enjoyment. Confidence remains a key issue for them.

AGE 35-44

- Most women at this stage now place a high amount of importance on their role as a mother.

AGE 45-54

- Many women of this age group place a high amount of importance on their relationship with their children, more so than any other age group.

AGE 55–64

- Their role as a mother continues to be important to many women in this age group.
- These women's contribution to society or a community also begins to become more important at this stage in their lives.

AGE 65 AND OVER

- Many of these women base their feelings of self-satisfaction on their contribution to society or their community. This is significantly greater than at any other stage of life.

What is clear is that, as women age, their sense of self and the way they view themselves starts as more internalised experiences of who they are and how they look and feel. As they age, their feelings of satisfaction about themselves shift into their roles with regard to other people, such as a partner or mother. In the later stages of their lives, women base their sense of self-satisfaction on their contribution to society or their community.

We can see in the results of thousands of surveys that there is a real shortfall in relation to mental health and confidence. The current constructs of life, work and society make women feel less than they hope or aspire to. This carries through to the respondents' sense that that they don't look and feel good. Sadly, women often believe that their work doesn't count and that they aren't making an impact at work.

A large part of how we feel about ourselves revolves around our confidence, which we have explored Part I of this book. When I met Katarina Johnson-Thompson, the world number-one-ranked heptathlete, she was a perfectly honed athlete at the peak of her career, but she explained that she used to define her self-worth by her achievements on the track. She then realised that she had to separate her work from her personal life and separate her expectations from other people's expectations. She told us that now, when she goes into an event, she knows what it's taken to get her there, and it's all about self-belief and focusing on what you need to do.

Many women, particularly in their middle years, will try to find confidence and happiness through their delivery of certain tasks or roles. They focus on their output rather than an internal feeling of confidence, and this can easily slip into traits of perfectionism and multitasking – if they can just get one more thing ticked off their to-do list they will feel better about themselves and finally feel happy. Women can often be reduced to lists, and lists are what wear us out.

Perfectionism is a common trait among women, much more so than men. It demands impossible standards and is often counterproductive as each task requires much more energy than might be necessary and it often hampers delegation. In a business sense, it can mean that women focus on the minutiae, but in business you are rarely remembered for the little things. No entrepreneur has ever been remembered for completing fourteen tasks in one day. Instead, they are remembered for their big, bold overarching plan.

In a recent poll on LinkedIn, we asked our audience, 'Do you consider yourself a perfectionist?' We received 52,290 votes, and the responses were:

- Yes: 56%
- No: 42%
- Other: 2%

Shortly afterwards we asked our audience, 'How do you view your perfectionism? Is it a positive or negative trait?' We received 27,718 votes, with the following replies:

- Positive: 36%
- Negative: 51%
- Other: 13%

Similarly, women can often strive to be multitaskers and see this as a superpower. Multitasking, like perfectionism, diffuses our energy, and is also a myth. Our brains cannot actually watch a film, read a book and have a conversation with our partner simultaneously; they can only focus on one source of information at a time. Multitasking is really juggling between different jobs and we end up doing all of them at a lower standard.

Our sense of self is also very much tied to our emotional state and how we process our feelings. As children, many young girls are taught to prioritise kindness over everything else. When we prioritise kindness, it can have a lifelong effect on how we view ourselves and our role in the world. For women, this means we can be steered into caring roles throughout our career, which also happen to be very low-paid. Society might say that kindness is one of the worthiest attributes, but it certainly doesn't pay wages to support that theory.

This desire to be kind can often mean that we also struggle to process emotions that are viewed as 'negative' ones, such as anger. Like all our emotions, anger is important, but generations of girls have been taught to suppress it. Anger tells us when our boundaries have been crossed, when we need to defend ourselves and when we are being treated unfairly. When we teach girls to suppress anger and instead turn to kindness it makes it more difficult for them to stand up for themselves. Conversely, when we allow ourselves to feel angry about the way we have been treated, especially if we have been treated unjustly, it can often be a greater motivator for success.

Feeling angry doesn't make you a bad person and many women suppress this emotion as they believe it does. Just because we suppress anger doesn't mean it will simply melt away. Instead, anger will remain there, underneath the surface, and can turn into passive-aggressive behaviour. This type of behaviour, where we don't verbalise that we feel wronged but show it in different ways or say unrelated things, destroys people because it stops them from being someone who people can trust. Passive-aggressive people are the ones who ask for feedback, but others instinctively know that they can't tell them the truth because they just want to hear sycophantic responses. Passive-aggressives will never say what has upset them, and will instead hide your stapler. Those around them will know they can't be trusted and, consequently, they will struggle to have meaningful relationships.

Tips: How to deal with anger

Anger can be a great motivator as it can push us to prove ourselves and achieve our goals. Life is often unfair, and that unfairness can be the driver that causes us to work harder and prove that we are as good as anyone else – and possibly better.

The last thing we want to do with anger is hide it and respond in a passive-aggressive way. When we don't express our anger, it eats away at us and weakens us. It is much better to explain why we are angry and how someone else's actions or words have made us feel that way.

If we do receive feedback that is unfairly negative this emotional response has to be dealt with and addressed. Logic is always a powerful ally, so it often helps to ask why someone thinks as they do and what is the evidence for how they think.

In a difficult situation which stimulates anger or frustration, there is a stereotypical truth that men tend to shout and express anger openly (and somewhat indiscriminately), whereas women may well resort to tears and crying. Women often turn their feelings in on themselves rather than pushing them out as men tend to do. Sometimes when we are angry there is an automatic trigger to cry as it's a way of releasing anger. I've heard from many people that one of the dreads as a female leader is crying in a public setting. What I have noticed is that to prevent this response, we have to allow the anger, or at least the logic of why we feel as we do, to come out and say exactly what is wrong about a situation.

If you are a leader and not allowed to ever be angry you will self-combust. You must be authentic and show how you feel – both the good and the bad. You will then learn to let it go and move on. Bearing grudges or worrying about what was said by you or others in the past is destructive and unhelpful. Something I admire in male leaders is that they push their anger out, release it and it's gone, whereas women can often draw their anger in.

When we respond with anger, we have two choices. We can either throw things up in the air or use our words to express our anger. Words will have more lasting power than an out of control display of anger. It's important for people around you, who have less power, to understand that you are angry with the situation or what they have done rather than being angry with them personally. When it comes to those around you who have power, they should understand how they have caused you to feel.

As the author and presenter, Katie Piper, once told us:

Mindset is key. I'm not a fluffy person. Being positive doesn't mean you have to be happy or cope all the time. Positive people can acknowledge all their emotions, are strong enough to experience them all and to be vulnerable. I've had some euphoric moments in my life. I've had dark moments when I've questioned why this is happening to me or my family. And then there are other moments when things are dull. I like the idea that you breathe in through the amazing parts, hold on through the awful, and breathe out and relax during the ordinary parts.

Anger might not mean that everyone will like you, but there is a good chance that people will respect you more than if you act in a passive-aggressive manner. As with most things, it is a fine balance and a lot depends on the type of relationship in which you are experiencing anger, whether it is with a colleague, boss, friend or partner. These relationships all create different impacts on our lives as we are required to play different roles, which we will explore more in Chapter 8.

Bobbi Brown, make-up artist, author, public speaker, entrepreneur and founder of Bobbi Brown Cosmetics

My mother was a knock-out – she was glamorous. It took me a long time to realise that, no matter what I did, I wasn't going to look just like her. Then, when I went into the fashion industry and was doing photo shoots with supermodels, I realised that at five feet tall, I wasn't going to be able to look like them either! I simply had to be me. That was a big, wonderful moment for me because it's when I became comfortable being myself. I realised that it's not about how you look. It's about how you feel you look, and that's such an important message.

Back when I launched Bobbi Brown Cosmetics, make-up was very heavy, artificial, brightly coloured and very garish. My message couldn't have been more different.

CHAPTER 8

RELATIONSHIPS

In general, women consistently rate their relationships as an area of high importance to them throughout their lifetime, and often above everything else. Over 44% of respondents gave Relationships as the most important pillar for them. Before diving into what this means, we need to clarify that when we talk about the term 'Relationships', it doesn't just mean our romantic ones. It encompasses all of the rich interactions we have in every area of our life, including the ones with our:

- Partner
- Parents
- Friends
- Colleagues
- Children
- Boss

Our relationships contain many elements, depending on their nature and whether they incorporate degrees of dependency. My husband Clive, and I are polar opposites. We have different skillsets, interests and ways of solving problems. As I've said before, with this powerful combination, you can achieve more than you would alone, but there also has to be something that bonds you to each other, such as your beliefs and values. In our example, we both work hard, and we respect that about each other. I don't think our relationship would have lasted if we thought the other was skiving their responsibilities. Instead, kindness and respect for each other's skills have held us together. Our brains are wired differently and we get annoyed with each other about the smaller, petty things in life, but not the big decisions. Our strategic partners used to call Clive 'the genius', but he always respected that I was the commercial decision-maker and would turn the ideas into a scalable financial model, with motivated and smart teams, in a way that he never could.

Independence is often key when it comes to our closest relationships. Katie Piper said something similar when we interviewed her:

> My belief is that as a woman it's very important to be independent. I want my girls not to have to rely on other people to feel complete – so that anyone who comes into their life is a welcome addition rather than a necessity to complete them, or being something they're waiting for in order to become themselves.

I agree wholeheartedly with Katie's approach about seeing ourselves as already complete. If the next generation of girls is raised this way, the foundations for empowerment will be in place.

When it comes to the caring element of our relationships, the data is clear that the burden of childcare and caring for relatives falls largely on women. The Centre for Progressive Policy carried out research published in 2021, which showed that women provided more than double the amount of unpaid childcare each year compared to men.[1]

Many mothers, and fathers, often realise they will have to perform a juggling act between having a career and being there when their children need them. We managed the baby-intense years in my household, despite huge work demands, because Clive and I agreed on a deal whereby we would take turns for one of us to be with the children when the other travelled for work. That kind of trust and reliance frees you up to do what you believe you were put on this planet to do. Being able to do a job that you love is hugely empowering. Doing it without guilt (well, mostly) is even better.

A lot has changed in recent decades around the distribution of childcare, and in general, men with children living at home contribute more to their children's care and household tasks than their fathers or grandfathers would have done. However, the balance is still uneven. The data shows that caring for others is still mainly seen as the women's role within relationships. As Dame Athene Donald, Professor of Experimental Physics and Master of Churchill College, astutely said, 'I do think that there is still a presumption among many people that childcare is the woman's problem, when it's not – it's the couple's problem.'

The 'caring role' impacts many areas of women's lives. As we saw in Chapter 7, women deprioritise their Self pillar once they enter these roles and focus on other people. It also has a far-reaching financial impact. When women are expected to provide unpaid care, it limits the amount of paid work they can do. This reduces the amount of money they earn, and their job is less lucrative than their partner's and seen as less important.

Consequently, when more care is required, women will be expected to provide this as they don't earn the same amount as their partner. It is cyclical and ultimately impacts how much money women can make in their lifetime, increasing women's 'money gap' with men. As a result, they are less financially prepared for the future, their pensions are lower and they are more likely to retire into poverty.

Men have children, and they have parents too, so why does this unpaid burden fall on women? Throughout the centuries, women have been taught to be nurturing and caring. At the same time, men have been expected to be the providers. In recent decades, most households require two salaries to stay afloat, but the role of 'carer' still lingers on as a female role rather than being evenly distributed. This can cause an unequal balance in what women put into their relationships, what they receive and what others expect of them.

When I met Juliet Stevenson, an Olivier-winning and BAFTA- and Olivier-nominated actor, it was so interesting to hear of her experience of combining motherhood and acting. She told us that, practically speaking, being a working actress and a mother is complicated.

Looking back now, if I have a regret, I think I worked too much. When my first child was born, three months later I whipped her into the car and we were off doing a huge series filming. I took a wonderful nanny with me but I now look back and think, 'God, did I miss all sorts of things?' I'm a very hands-on mother. I always wanted to have kids and I have adored all of it, including the challenges. That's probably the most important part of my life.

Looking back, I think being a parent actually really helps the work. I think psychologically it's made me much more stable; if I hadn't had children, I would have been much more vulnerable to the profession eating me away, eating me up. The frailties, the nervousness, the sense of insecurity, they constantly feed on you – I have often rooted myself back at home with the kids, and then none of it matters very much. What they are doing, who they are turning out to be, what they need day by day, are the really important things. The bruising of the profession, and even the triumphs, are pushed into perspective by them. Children keep you rooted and earthed.

There is also a distorted view on the contribution women and men provide to consider. Research from the University of Chicago shows that mothers are more likely to say they do more of the household responsibilities. In contrast, men are more likely to say that they share them.[2] Similarly, an increase in sharing household responsibilities in mixed-sex couples with children during the Covid-19 lockdowns was reported, but this then returned to pre-pandemic levels, according to research published in 2021.[3] Interestingly, this study showed that mixed-sex couples without children are more likely to still be sharing the housework equally.

There is also the organisation around the caring role to consider. At The Female Lead, we call this the 'mental load', which is a psychological condition that has been revealed and explored by one of the psychologists we work with, Dr Terri Apter. The mental load encompasses all the jobs that keep a household running that often go unseen and unrecognised. It is a condition that also contributes towards explaining why women suffer burnout, because they worry about all the jobs that need doing and plan every day throughout the year. Even if men help out in the house, women largely organise what needs doing and when.

This isn't always the case in every single household, of course. Ashleigh Linsdell, who is a nurse and founder of For the Love of Scrubs, told us that her husband supports her in ways that she never thought possible. He does a huge amount of childcare and in her family childcare is definitely not the woman's job. He has cooked her roast dinners after she's finished nights, and stayed up until the middle of the night to make sure her work uniform is washed, dried and ironed for the following day. She explained that when she's in the middle of her fourth night shift in a row and she's freezing and exhausted, knowing that she's not doing it alone and she has support at home is how she gets through it.

The cost of childcare also has to be considered. Recent results from the Organisation for Economic Co-operation and Development (OECD) found that the UK has one of the highest childcare costs in the world.[4] In England, according to research by Business in the Community (BITC), this means that the average nursery fees for the under-twos takes 65% of a parent's average wage.[5]

The issue of childcare requires governmental change as it is not a problem that women can or should be expected to fix by themselves. The same research by the Centre of Progressive Policy showed that the cost of childcare prevented 1.3 million women from having a job and 1.7 million women from taking on extra working hours.[6] This is also not a problem that falls at the feet of childcare providers as they are being squeezed by their own running costs. This leaves us in a place where our governments have to choose whether they want couples to work or not. If they want couples to work, they will have to provide good-quality childcare for a lower cost through increased grants to working parents. If governments want to release women's economic power and the sense of fulfilment they get from work, then good childcare is fundamental.

There is also a lot of divisive language and potentially judgemental behaviour when it comes to women returning to work and around motherhood in general. When we hear about women returning to work, they often 'leave their children' in order to do this. It's very emotive language and rarely applied to men. Instead, men 'provide' for their children when they return to work after paternity leave.

This divisive language stretches throughout women's lives as mothers, as Judy Murray, the former Scottish Number One tennis player and Scotland's National Coach experienced. She told me that as a tennis parent, it's easy to become overinvested in your child because you are putting in so much time, money and effort to help them improve. But because she was the national coach, she didn't get so caught up with her own kids, Andy and Jamie Murray. Wimbledon in 2005 was a rude awakening for her. It was Andy's breakthrough year and suddenly the media got very excited about Judy sitting in the players' box and she was picked out on television. She knew that there was sexism in opinion pieces about her. She felt that if she had been the dad of two competitive sons who were starting to find their way into the spotlight, she would have been lauded and applauded – instead, she was viewed as the pushy, overbearing mum.

* * *

If our thirties and forties often revolve around caring for our young, the decades after this can incorporate caring for our older relatives. According to the Office for National Statistics (ONS), around 2 million adults in the UK are receiving informal care, and older workers in their 50s and 60s are most likely to provide this care.[7] As with childcare, this is split unevenly between men and women, with one in four older female workers providing this care, whereas the figure is one in eight for older male workers. This research only incorporates people who are working. When we take into account people who are not working in these age groups, these figures might be much higher. Because women are having children later in their lifetimes, many women find themselves caring for children and shortly afterwards, or even simultaneously, moving straight into the role of being a carer for elderly relatives.

Tips: Handling office politics

There was a time when I used to say that I didn't 'do' office politics. I thought my ideas and work would make me stand out and be seen as a shining beacon of perfection and transformation without any support or communication. How wrong I was. I soon realised that not doing office politics was a bit naive and a purist statement, as office politics aren't always negative. I hadn't worked out how to be me and fit in well with the style and complexity of the organisation I was working for. I realised that I needed to respect the company where I worked and learn to communicate my work and contribution in as many ways and through as many leaders as necessary to make progress. So, my simple checklist became this:

- Take time to understand how your organisation works and how decisions are made.
- Observe the formal and informal sessions where opinion and influence are discussed and evaluated. Be prepared to invest more than just standard meetings and working hours.
- Recognise that you have a role in learning to navigate the organisation, who you will need to influence and how you can do this both before and after a key event.

- Not all office politics are toxic. They can be positive as well. Fitting in with a distinctive corporate culture and style makes it easier to work out how you or your team can be in the right place at the right time, in order to show what you think or what you can do.
- Be willing to invest the time and overcome the frustration that sometimes comes when you don't get your way the first time around. Be open, ask questions and be respectful of others' opinions.
- If your boss doesn't understand the importance of what you're saying or doing, it may be because you're not explaining clearly or showcasing your ideas.
- Don't be defensive or aggressive if people look like they are blocking you or your idea. Instead, ask them what their objections are because they can be a step forward when they are understood properly. This can help you turn a negative into a positive.

Nadia Murad, Nobel Peace Prize Laureate and UNODC Goodwill Ambassador

Growing up, my mother was my world. She taught me to be strong and speak my mind. She was smart, caring and never stopped working to build a better life for our family. My mother made me who I am today. She taught me about resilience, independence and courage. I miss her every day.

HOW THE IMPORTANCE OF RELATIONSHIPS CHANGES AS WE AGE

Relationships are the most important area to women's fulfilment overall throughout their lifetime (see Figure 8.1). The importance of relationships peaks slightly between the ages of 25 and 34 and gradually decreases as women progress through the later stages of life. Furthermore, the overall variation by age is much lower than all other pillars.

The peak (shown in Figure 8.1) representing women in their late twenties reflects a time when women are often navigating the different types of relationships that begin to develop during this stage of their lives, such as with bosses, partners, children and colleagues.

From a persona point of view, perhaps not surprisingly, the Relationship pillar shows a stronger correlation with those personas associated with team-working, such as Everyone's Friend, Entertainer and Mediator.

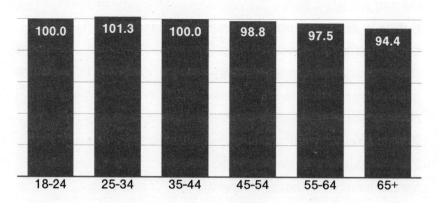

Figure 8.1. Relative Importance of Relationships.

HOW THE IMPORTANCE OF RELATIONSHIPS CHANGES DEPENDING ON OUR PERSONAL CIRCUMSTANCES

When it comes to feeling fulfilled, many married women's relationships are significantly more important to them than their money or sense of self, especially if children are present in the home. They also generally care more about relationships than other women and rate this as the highest pillar of importance. Similarly, women who are breadwinners also rank their relationships as their most important area of fulfilment. The emotional drivers behind these show that married women prioritise feelings of connectedness. In contrast, women who are breadwinners place importance on the feeling of power, followed closely by control.

Many women who are part of an ethnic minority in the country where they live rate relationships as least important to them. Single women do the same, and focus on their sense of self.

When it comes to the variability of the results, most replies exist in a narrow band. The average scores vary little by age or location. The responses are also consistent across most countries, with the exceptions of India and France where Relationships come second to Self as a key pillar. Over 49% of respondents in Sweden ranked the Relationship pillar as the most important, compared to just 31.3% in India. The United Kingdom, New Zealand and Ireland all also scored well above average for the Relationship pillar, whereas the bottom three countries were Switzerland, and then by large measure, France and India at 33.2% and 31.3%, respectively. In these two countries, the Self pillar is more important to women than Relationships and in France the Relationships pillar falls to third place behind Self and Health.

THE TOPICS OF MOST IMPORTANCE WITHIN THE RELATIONSHIPS PILLAR BY AGE GROUP

The types of relationships that vary most with age within the Relationships pillar are, perhaps not surprisingly, partners, parents, friends and children. Whereas work colleagues and bosses or managers tend to be fairly consistent for all ages.

When we explore the gap between actual recorded measures of women's fulfilment in their relationships and where women would like or expect to be, generally, this gap is smallest between parents in relation to their children. It is at its highest with partner relationships. The key takeaways for each age group are:

AGE 18–24

- Friendships are the most important relationship to this age group's fulfilment in this area.

AGE 25–34

- Friends remain a key relationship, but the expectation of their partner grows.
- They are most satisfied with the relationships they have with their friends.

- Women of this age group lack feelings of power in their relationships but are generally satisfied emotionally in relationships at this stage of their lives.

AGE 35-44

- Relationships with their children have now become a priority for this age group.

AGE 45-54

- For this age group, relationships with their children are the most important ones. They are also the ones that are most generally satisfied when it comes to their relationship fulfilment.

AGE 55-64

- Women of this age group have the most significant satisfaction gap when it comes to the relationship they have with their partner. This means there is the largest gap between where they want their relationship fulfilment to be and how they currently rate it.

AGE 65 AND OVER

- Relationships with colleagues and ex-colleagues are the most important ones to many women of this age group, more so than women of any other age group. However, this may be distorted now that relationships with their parents become less likely and so the score here logically plummets, and there is a marked decline in the score for partners too.

Our data shows that out of all the relationships women have, the one with their partner or spouse has the most significant gap between what women expect or aspire to and the reality of what they have. However, this varies a lot by age. The relationship with a partner or spouse is perhaps the most complex and important one women have. Women's resilience in these relationships is evident and shows a keen awareness and expectation that it needs to be strong. The relationship measure most aligned with expectation is a woman's relationship with her boss. This doesn't mean that it is the most fulfilling relationship. Instead, it means that women's expectations of this type of relationship are most closely aligned with what they experience.

*   *   *

Women's relationships are consistently crucial to them throughout their lives, although the type of relationship they rate as most important to them changes as they age. The next pillar we will be exploring is the Health pillar, which fluctuates very differently depending on our circumstances and age.

Tova Leigh, author, actress and blogger

I had my first daughter when I was 35. For me motherhood didn't come naturally. It's hard to admit that because we are told from an early age that motherhood is our goal. That no matter what else you do, you are going to get to motherhood. That isn't true. Being a mother didn't feel like I thought it would and that was a real shock. I had post-partum depression and only years later did I realise. It's so important to recognise the symptoms.

My twins came less than two years later. Having three children in the space of two years is massive. There aren't words to describe how deeply I felt I was drowning. But there are no people I love more than my daughters; it had nothing to do with them, it was to do with me. The expectation that the mum drops out of her career to raise the family is a major factor in gender inequality. I automatically stopped work. It was not a conversation we had. Now when I look back, I think, 'How did that happen?'

One day I snapped and needed to vent. I wrote what ended up being my first blog. Then I started writing on a regular basis and then making vlogs. That's when it kind of exploded. At first there wasn't a goal in my content, apart from letting mothers, and parents in general, know that they're not alone. I was opening a door for parents to say that they were struggling. I tried to make it funny too and it helped me; it was almost therapeutic. Then my work became more about women. I wanted to break down the boundaries and stereotypes. To say that there's no one way to be a woman or a mother. There is no one way to live your life.

CHAPTER 9

HEALTH

Unlike most of the other pillars, the Health pillar does not rise or fall sharply in importance as we grow older. Rather, its importance increases over the years as a natural response to most people's declining health as they age. It is also the most volatile of the pillars. This is probably because when we are impacted by health issues, it shoots up our personal priority list and trumps all other issues. If we are lucky enough not to experience health issues, it remains of lower concern and priority.

This has been my experience as well. I never really thought about my health until I could not work for three months because of glandular fever. I was around 24 years old, newly married and thought the department I ran would collapse without me. It was an important lesson because I learned that life goes on and people step in and up. The system I had established ensured I wasn't irreplaceable. When I returned to work, my health worries slowly faded into the background again, and I continued to expect my body to keep pace with the demands I placed on it.

That continued until I turned 50 when I was suddenly and shockingly diagnosed with breast cancer. This is something I have never spoken publicly about until now. I was CEO of a 1,500-strong company and decided to share this information with my team, leadership and our special joint-venture retail partners. I felt intensely vulnerable and was very concerned about the stability of the business. I wanted to crawl into a hole and remain silent until I was fixed. I wanted to hold my breath and prayed I would live. My children were my number one priority and concern. The world drops from underneath when you are diagnosed with something life-threatening like cancer. Your priorities flip instantly, and it's a real wake-up call. That year was the worst of my life.

I decided to step away from work for six months to focus on my health and the treatment I would be going through. Leaving my work behind was terrifying as I worried about whether the business would survive and everyone would be alright. However, what it actually showed me was that I had a fantastic team of people who were clever, loyal and kind. I discovered we'd built a solid support system and I had a group of close colleagues and friends at work who rallied around, stepped up and stepped forward. I'd always believed in the Power of Two, and at that moment, I realised that there were so many more people in that relationship than just Clive and me.

When I returned after six months, I was still receiving treatment, but everyone was so supportive. All my fears about dying from cancer and the business collapsing receded slowly. I found that when you face your worst fears, a huge strength follows. You've survived. I took this strength, what I had learned about myself, and the phenomenal team around me, my brilliant husband and my young and extended family and used it to move forward. When it comes to our health in conjunction with work, we need to grant ourselves and others permission to be unwell.

I was hypersensitive at the time to others seeing me as weak and failing, but perhaps that was just in my mind. However, I have known some incredibly senior male leaders who have never spoken of their journey when they faced a similar health horror. We all approach our health differently and find many helpful ways to process ill health. When Victoria Derbyshire discovered she had breast cancer she decided to record her treatment through the cancer, because she's a journalist.

I approached it factually: this is what happens when you have a mastectomy; this is what happens when you have chemotherapy. Obviously going through this treatment, there were lows. I thought: *OK, I've got to be honest about this, how I am affected by this treatment and the side-effects* – my hair falling out or feeling incredibly low because chemotherapy wipes you out. Or how I felt about losing a breast. As it happens, I was more distressed about losing my hair than losing a breast because I thought, *I just want the cancer out of me.* I felt it helped me continue to be a journalist and not only to be a cancer patient.

The Health pillar also incorporates the health of those around us, not just our own. The social justice campaigner, Gina Miller, told us about the experience of her daughter being starved of oxygen at birth and being told that she should send her away to an institution.

The lioness in me awoke. I fought my ex-husband, her father; I fought the institutions, I fought the doctors, I fought the authorities and I kept her. Part of my battle was also ensuring that all parents could keep their children and get special support through the educational system.

As this is a book about women, we should also say that when we talk about the Health pillar, it doesn't just mean women's health issues such as periods, fertility and childbirth, although these topics do make an appearance throughout different stages of women's lives. Instead, the Health pillar of fulfilment incorporates:

- Physical health
- Female health, such as fertility and menopause
- Family health
- Preventative health
- Holistic
- Mental health

We have probably all heard of the gender pay gap, but there is a gender health gap as well. Various research has been done on this, and it has even been debated in the House of Lords. A study by University College London found that women with dementia in the UK receive worse healthcare than men.[1] These women also visit the GP less than men, receive less healthcare monitoring and are prescribed more potentially harmful medication. Similarly, research by the University of Toronto has shown that in a patient sample of 1.3 million, when operated on by a male surgeon, women had a 14.9% increase of a bad outcome compared to when a female surgeon operated on them.[2] Conversely, men had similar results regardless of whether a man or a woman operated on them. The gender health gap also increases if the women are from minority backgrounds or deprived areas. For example, research shows that black women are 40% more likely to miscarry than white women in the UK.[3]

When it comes to women's health, there has been a welcome increase in open discussion about it in recent years, but little investment in the healthcare that women require to deal with it. As with many conditions that fall under 'female health', there is often a solution that is not as readily available as it should be, such as women's access to Hormone Replacement Therapy (HRT). This leaves women in the position that men are more aware of female health issues and often read about the extremes of these cases in the media, but they are unaware of how many relatively simple solutions would be available to women if the funding were put in place.

If men only hear about the extremes of female health through the media rather than about average experiences through conversations with women, it also places many women in the situation of being classified as a series of biological processes and stereotypes that they then become governed by: waiting to become a woman, puberty, making sure they don't get pregnant, making sure they do get pregnant, the pregnancy and childbirth years, peri-menopause, menopause and finally postmenopause. When women are viewed in this way, it takes away their individual experiences, outlooks and the importance they, as individuals, place on these changes. It casts women as a series of biological processes that workplaces have to deal with, while sucking out some of the joy of just *living* if women are continuously on alert for the next biological 'event' that is now heralded by a series of presumed failures and faults.

Women are not a series of biological traumas but, if we are viewed as this, we are labelled and often judged inadequate without ever really being seen. We also need to talk about the average experiences while getting into place the healthcare that can help women across the board.

Tips: How to avoid burnout

Burnout is common in the high-pressure working lives so many of us have. I have always worked in these potentially derailing situations and have managed to avoid burnout by doing the following:

- Running a business is a marathon, not a sprint, and so is any career. You will quickly exhaust all your reserves if you continuously treat each new project or role as a 100-metre dash.
- It is usual to have ups and downs in all jobs, but if you are continuously not enjoying it, you are in the wrong job. Not being in a role that suits us will erode our happiness and self-worth.
- If you can have fun at your job, even if you're working hard, it will lower your stress levels. Humour and laughing with colleagues and sometimes at yourself breaks up the heavy pace that can lead to burnout.
- It's essential to have something else in your life that makes you want to stop working for a while, such as family, friends or children. Children can be exhausting, but they are a different type of exhausting.
- Try to have one thing you can do by yourself that is unconnected to your work. It should be something gentle like gardening, which will give you the time for all the adrenaline to drain out of you.
- On social media, we might see mums who are career women and also seem to be going out every night to a different event. In reality, we can probably only do one or two of these things,

as there are only so many roles we can perform. Women who manage all three probably also have multiple nannies!

- Ultimately, exhaustion and burnout happen when we keep on taking energy and reserves from ourselves without putting anything back in. We need to take time to refill those reserves so we can continue with the marathon.

HOW THE IMPORTANCE OF HEALTH CHANGES AS WE AGE

Health is the third most important area, on average, to women's overall fulfilment throughout their lifetimes (see Figure 9.1). The importance of this area grows steadily as we age, and there are no sudden uplifts or drops as we sometimes see in the other pillars.

Overall, Health is ranked as the third most important pillar, but it rapidly overtakes Self as women reach their forties. When

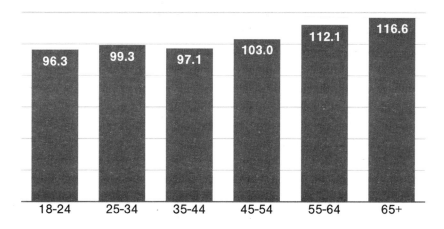

Figure 9.1. Relative importance of Health.

women reach their sixties, it becomes the most important pillar. Health is a very important pillar for Creators and Bon Vivant personas, but much less important for Achievers.

> **Vanessa Xuereb, Chief Membership Officer at Soho House Group**
>
> I don't fully remember my youth because, at the age of 21, I suffered a head injury after being hit by a car. I lost all of my memory. After the injury, I had to relearn everything: people's names, where I met them, what had happened. I even forgot how to drive. The head injury changed my life, I couldn't walk for about three months and had a whole host of problems. I was really unwell for about two years and had very bad PTSD. I also had a stutter and lost all of my confidence. I relied on my friends and family to tell me what had happened. After the accident, it made me value every moment even more – because my life changed in a split second and I'm just very lucky that I came out if it.

HOW THE IMPORTANCE OF HEALTH CHANGES DEPENDING ON OUR PERSONAL CIRCUMSTANCES

Health isn't considered the most important pillar area by any of the groups we categorise women into, depending on their circumstances. It is regarded as the least important area by women who earn their own money but live in shared occupancy.

Although Health is the third most important pillar, it is also the most volatile one with a wide range of responses. This perhaps reflects the fact that if Health is a current issue for a person or their family it features much more highly as a key concern. However, despite the range of responses, it is reasonably consistent across the countries we gathered data on. Geographically, Health is of particular importance to the French, where it ranks second to Self. It is also important to the Swiss, for whom Health is rated higher than Self, and is second only to Relationships. Health scores lowest in the UK, USA, New Zealand and Ireland.

THE TOPICS OF MOST IMPORTANCE WITHIN THE HEALTH PILLAR BY AGE GROUP

The scores in this pillar were highest for the topics of personal mental health and physical health, followed by the same issues for family members. Both of these were a long way ahead of preventative screening or healthcare systems for our respondents. Healthy eating, nutrition and physical activity showed the biggest variation for those people who ranked health as their top priority, whereas the core concern for most women is mental wellness. Overall, the lowest scoring area was fertility, though this was an important area of concern for younger women. Menopause and ageing showed the widest variations, being of concern to women over the age of 45.

The biggest variations when we looked at people who ranked the Health pillar as the most important area to them was in physical health, whereas the health of partners for these people was seen as much less important. This suggests that a key reason for ranking this pillar highly is the personal circumstances of the individual. The key takeaways for each age group are:

AGE 18–24

- They care about sexual health more than any other age group.
- They are also particularly concerned about mental health and the gap between the strength and confidence they would like to feel and where they currently see themselves. This reflects many of the anxieties we have seen in our research for these younger women, particularly when a lot of time is spent scrolling passively on social platforms.

Dr Julie Smith, who is a clinical psychologist and online educator, told us how she has helped younger people access tools to help them with their mental health. It began when she was working as a clinical psychologist and noticed that a lot of the young people coming to her didn't really need long-term therapy.

She explained that a part of therapy is educational: you teach people how the mind works, how to influence mood and manage emotions. A lot of people, once they had that information, were ready to go. They found it empowering and she kept talking to people about how it should be made available and should be free, as they shouldn't have to see a therapist to find out simple life skills. So, she and her husband decided to help with this and started making YouTube videos. It was when they found TikTok and tried to make some really short snappy videos that it took off. It turned out that people were really hungry for that information.

Julie told us that her wish is that people know that they have more influence over how they feel. She explained that people think that if they don't feel happy all the time, it's a weakness or something they're getting wrong, but actually it is a normal part of being human. There are lots of really simple ways we can influence how we feel. She wants people to have information that is empowering to them to help them make life a bit easier.

AGE 25-34

- Fertility and pregnancy are more important than other health areas to many women in this age group. They also place more importance on this than any other age group.

AGE 35-44

- In this age group, the health of their family becomes a priority.
- Many of these women also have a large satisfaction gap when it comes to how they feel about their health.

AGE 45-54

- Arranging regular, preventative screenings now becomes important to many of these women.
- Menopause and ageing are most important, more so than any other age group, and they feel a large gap in satisfaction in this area.
- Women of this age group also lack feelings of power regarding their health.

AGE 55-64

- Health now becomes a priority, especially preventative health.
- Menopause and ageing continue to be an important consideration, although the satisfaction gap for these women is less than for women who are slightly younger. This may reflect the fact that menopause, while viewed as a key issue, can be an expected and accepted challenge, especially when society's lack of understanding of and support for it is a reality in our current environment.

AGE 65 AND OVER

- Arranging preventative screenings is of high importance to many women at this stage of their lives.
- They also begin to place more importance again on getting support from their healthcare system.
- They also turn to holistic and alternative therapies and become more anxious about access to healthcare.

Sheryl Crow, singer and winner of nine Grammy awards, once said that unless you really have the strength and the fortitude to allow yourself to age, it can be devastating to have society decide what roles you should be playing and what clothes you should be wearing. She went on to say that as women we suffer being disqualified as we get old, but that ageing is something to be honoured and celebrated, as opposed to being fixed. She firmly believes that you have to embrace and own the beautiful aspects of getting older and wiser.

As women age, they naturally focus on different areas of their health. In their younger years, they are concerned about their sexual health more than any other age group before moving on to fertility and pregnancy. Similar to what we have seen with the Self pillar, women then focus on the health of those in their family and deprioritise their own health. When women are aged 45–54, they begin to focus on preventative screening and are much more aware of ageing. Menopause is also another important topic to them. As they move into the next age bracket, these topics are still of importance, but women feel less expectation around this and more acceptance, which is shown by a lower satisfaction gap. In the last age group, preventative screenings are still important, alongside disease management.

Overall, Health takes on a clear focus and concern for all women. It highlights that there is now a lot of attention on mental wellness and a concern around physical activity and fitness. The importance of Health is even stronger and more defined by age and where women have direct worries or concerns. The topic that is of least general concern is fertility and pregnancy, although we know that as many women increasingly delay parenthood, women are looking to discover new ways to protect against infertility challenges in later years.

There is the other side of our health to consider as well, which is our mental health. When it comes to depression, there is a gender gap here as well. According to the World Health Organization, women are 50% more likely to suffer from depression than men. The reason for this gap isn't solely due to biology either.[4] Many of the factors we have discussed, such as inequality in power and status and the burden of the mental load, contribute to women's increased risk of depression. Depression can often be a rational response to outside factors from society, family circumstances, caring responsibilities and relationships. There is even research that shows that in the UK women are significantly unhappier than men, leading to more days with poor mental health and restless sleep.[5]

There are also significant barriers to women accessing treatment for addiction. Research from the charity Be Gamble Aware shows that 39% of women experiencing high levels of harm from gambling are reluctant to seek help because they are worried about stigma, feel embarrassed or don't want people to know about it.[6] Across all types of addictions, women with children often refrain from seeking help because they are worried about alerting social services to their situation.

There are also eating disorders to consider, and how they affect women disproportionately over men. Megan Jayne Crabbe, author, digital creator and presenter, told us about her experience with this.

I struggled with eating disorders until I was 16. After that I dieted. I didn't escape from everything being about my body until I was 21 and found the body positive movement. I was scrolling through Instagram one day looking at Fitspo and supermodels, and I found the opposite: a bunch of people finding happiness in something other than what their bodies looked like. Until then, I'd lived my whole life believing that there was only one way to be happy and good enough – and suddenly there were these people forcing me to ask: what if that wasn't true? If it was possible to find happiness and fulfilment by changing my body, how come it hadn't happened yet? I'd been every size under the sun. I'd done every diet imaginable. I'd changed and moulded myself, and it hadn't worked.

The inequality of the gender health gap is a residual impact from women's health (and lives) being viewed historically as less important than men's and, in some circumstances, still being seen this way. It is also compounded by several factors, including a lack of research into women's health, fewer female study participants than male ones and a lack of funding for research into women's health.

Inequality in the 21st century often results from several underlying factors that feed into the main problem. In Chapter 10, we explore the contributing aspects around women's work that have left us with a significant gender pay gap despite the Equal Pay Act coming into force in the UK nearly 50 years ago.

Katie Piper, author, presenter and philanthropist
At the Katie Piper Foundation, the charity I set up to support burns rehabilitation and scar management for UK survivors, there's the physical side of burns treatment and there's also a social and wellbeing side. After acute care, we help people rebuild their lives to the standard they want. It's not just about going back to normal, it's about empowering them to be whatever they want to be after the injury. My long-term hope is that one day we won't be needed because burns and scars are accepted as part of life, that they're not a reason to ostracise somebody or assume they're not up to the job when they come for an interview, or find them unattractive because they're different and the media tells us that only symmetry is appealing.

CHAPTER 10

WORK

Inequality exists and is not imagined. When women face inequality, what happens in the workplace often has the most visible and corroborating data. The data and evidence gathered by independent researchers every year confirms the fact that women are consistently paid less than men. The gender pay gap is often discussed and, according to the Office for National Statistics, in 2022 there was a 14.9% difference between men and women for all employees in the UK.[1] In 2019, the Institute for Fiscal Studies held this discrepancy at 19% for an average hourly rate.[2] What is more alarming is that the same research found that the gender pay gap has only closed by 1.5% since 2005, and any progress that has happened is due to women attaining higher levels of education over that time. As Victoria Derbyshire says, 'Earning a wage means that you have independence, it means that you have options, it means you can provide for your family. It means the same for women as it means for men, so pay us equally.'

In the USA, the gender pay gap stands at similar levels, with women earning 82% of what men did in 2022.[3] This same research also confirms that the gender pay gap has barely moved in 20 years, having previously stood at 80% in 2002. Globally, the gender pay gap stands at women earning around 20%less than men.[4]

Within the Work pillar of fulfilment there are several topics, which include:

- Promotion and career development
- Fair pay
- Flexible working
- Maternity and childcare support
- Leadership support
- Mentor support

When we interviewed the freestyle footballer, Liv Cooke, she had a really strong and inspiring message on her view on money. She told us:

I like to make money, unapologetically. I've been on shoots where they've talked down about a woman who's wearing lots of jewellery or drives a flashy car, but then a man's praised. Why is that a thing? I just wish for a world where a girl can drive a Lamborghini and not be asked if her dad bought it. Or where a woman can be a CEO and sign deals and tell people what to do without being called bossy. Or where we can just chase our dreams. It's what we deserve. I'm not asking to be given extra credit or be paid more than a man. I'm just asking for equality.

Worldwide, the gender pay gap is clearly persistent and not closing quickly enough. In recent years it has been repeatedly highlighted and discussed, but little has changed. The difficulty with the gender pay gap is that it doesn't stem solely from women simply being paid less per hour than men, but from a myriad of factors arising from the construct of our workplaces. This is because, in most settings, the workplace is designed by men for men. The workplace is an old set-up and usually not fit for purpose for both women and men because if women are excluded from some of that environment, men currently often feel trapped by it.

The rigidity of the workplace does not accommodate women's differing circumstances, areas of fulfilment and the changes that occur during their lifetimes. Women are not two-dimensional caricatures of the average housewife or the alpha female. What we want from life changes as we grow from childhood into puberty and fertility and whether we want to have children or not, then on to family or carer demands, menopause and finally retirement. Women want and need different support at different stages in their life. As Bobbi Brown told us:

Men don't have to balance the same things as women do. Even if you're a high-powered woman, you have a lot to balance. Men don't have to worry about that. Being thoughtful and smart is what's going to make the biggest difference.

The irony is that consumer brands worked out a long time ago that women want different things at different stages of their lives and I was there to witness it. They use data and segmentation to understand which products and services we want through each of these stages. They apply sophisticated analysis research and planning to understand and respond to this, and their market research and consumer targeting sets one brand apart from another. It is because of these techniques that some brands are so attractive to certain demographic groups. And yet our workplace policies are lagging far behind.

When we join work we are all living in different circumstances, but we are all subject to the same policies. Organisations take a very simplistic view, and have created policies and procedures that apply to every employee - one size fits all. Just as consumer brands are used to the fact that consumers are different, our governments and businesses must also recognise that employees are as well. Employees want and need different things from work and require differing support at all ages and life stages. Our fulfilment - why we come to work - differs from other employees. This is the true meaning of *neurodiversity*, because what excites and motivates us can be radically different for someone else. In fact, we have more in common with men who have a similar work motivation than we do with women who have different motivations and drivers around their sense of fulfilment.

Once you understand a person, you can use data to show their motivation for going to work, and I always considered this when it came to my own company. For some people, it is about being a breadwinner. For many, it is because their friends are there, and for others, it is because they want to make an impact or be noticed making a difference. Once you know the motivation, you can adjust policies to meet these motivations and hopefully have an engaged workforce. Businesses are now worried that women are leaving the workplace in their millions, which has been termed the 'Great Resignation'. Employers don't understand what is causing it, so they are throwing benefits at employees to try and resolve the problem without truly understanding it. Sometimes the problem might be how workers are spoken to or treated. It might be flexibility or autonomy, or it might be benefits and money. Money is rarely unimportant to employees, but it's not always the most crucial contributory factor.

Employers generally treat all of us - men and women - as one homogenous group. For a long time, I have known that we need to apply a more sophisticated science, using data and research, to understand the motivations and needs of women. Only by better understanding and responding to their needs can we help realise their true potential and maximise women's role and economic contribution to society. If we highlight that women want different things from work and understand their motivation for going to work, then businesses will understand how they can relate better to employees and keep them through all the phases that women, in particular, go through. That would create a significant change in our world. Because if businesses could keep female workers throughout the different stages of their lives, it would have a major impact on keeping women in the workforce and therefore making a massive contribution to the economic strength of this country.

In a recent poll on LinkedIn, we asked our audience, 'How have childcare costs affected your working hours?' We received 11,732 votes, and the responses were:

- No impact on working hours: 46%
- Reduced hours: 26%
- Switched to part-time: 15%
- Quit job, stayed at home: 12%

(Responses rounded up or down by LinkedIn: 1%)

You might look at this data and pay attention to the largest number, which is that there has been no impact on working hours.

> But adding up the other three responses shows that childcare costs have affected 53% of respondents' working hours.

Our requirements in the workplace change throughout our lifetimes and according to our circumstances, and the data we have collected can help explain this.

HOW THE IMPORTANCE OF WORK CHANGES AS WE AGE

Work is the fourth most important area, on average, for women's overall fulfilment throughout their lifetime. The importance of this area grows in women's younger years and peaks at the middle stage of women's lives at age 35–44. As women age out of the workforce, the overall importance of this area declines until it drops to its lowest levels at age 65 and over (see Figure 10.1).

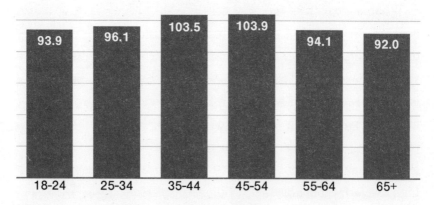

Figure 10.1. Relative importance of Work.

The Work pillar of fulfilment doesn't make an appearance as one of the most prioritised pillars until the age of 35–44, when it replaces relationships as the second most popular response, just below money. Interestingly, work remains the second most common pillar into the next age bracket of 45–54 before disappearing from the results as a most prioritised pillar.

From a persona perspective, the Work pillar is most associated with Achievers, Investigators and Reformers and is of low importance to Entertainers and Everyone's Friend.

HOW THE IMPORTANCE OF WORK CHANGES DEPENDING ON OUR PERSONAL CIRCUMSTANCES

Our survey responses can sometimes be surprising and this is highlighted when considering the responses from women with children. Although Work is still the fourth pillar overall for this group, they rate it more important than women without children or where the children have left home.

What is clear from our 'Unentitled Mindset' research, which is covered on page 171, is that fulfilment for working women is driven primarily by emotions of enjoyment and happiness and a sense of power from feeling confident and successful. Therefore, it is a mistake for employers to think that women with children are less interested in their work or find less enjoyment in it. The Work pillar also comes up as the most important pillar for women with shared financial responsibility, who, like married women, place a high level of importance on feeling connected.

The circumstances where the Work pillar comes up as least important are for women without children and women who aren't breadwinners.

When it comes to the volatility of the responses we received, geography plays a big part in its importance. Geographically, India scores Work highly. In contrast, Work scores poorly in Sweden and the Netherlands.

THE TOPICS OF MOST IMPORTANCE WITHIN THE WORK PILLAR BY AGE GROUP

Fair pay stands out as a key topic for this pillar, followed by flexible working, support from leadership, and promotion or career development. Networks, childcare provision and maternity support are less important to respondents. The smallest gaps between what women expect and what they feel they experience are in these areas too, where legislation has mostly set a core agenda for provision. Flexible working shows a very modest gap between expectation and experience, which suggests that it meets the demands of women. However, The Female Lead has identified a challenge around flexible working that lies ahead, which has been dubbed 'the Invisible Worker', which we will discuss further on in our research on this topic.

The largest fulfilment gap women experience is in relation to fair pay, which considerably eclipses the other areas of concern such as leadership support, career development and mentoring. The key takeaways for each age group are:

AGE 18-24

- Fair pay is extremely important to many women aged 18-24.

AGE 25-34

- Return to work and maternity support, as well as childcare, are more important to many women at this stage of life – more so than any other age group, which is perhaps not surprising.

AGE 35-44

- When it comes to work, many women's priorities shift to that of childcare provision at this stage of their lives.
- Of all the age groups, these women feel the most emotionally satisfied when it comes to work; however they do want to feel slightly more in control.

AGE 45-54

- This group of women finds the gap between expectation from work and current fulfilment much lower than younger age groups, with the exception of support from management.
- Each of the issues is of roughly equal consideration, but the gap between expectation and what they experience is much lower.

AGE 55-64

- Networking and mentoring becomes a bigger issue for this group of women.

- They are also looking for a higher degree of flexibility in their working lives.
- Again, the gap between expectation and what they experience continues to narrow.

AGE 65 AND OVER

- Flexible working continues to be important at this stage in life.
- However, many of these women have a large satisfaction gap when it comes to fair pay, suggesting that women of this age group are more likely to believe that they are being underpaid.

Women begin their working lives by being concerned with fair pay within this pillar. As they age and more women have children, this shifts to priorities around returning to work after pregnancy and maternity support. In general, at age 35–44, the focus for most women moves to childcare provision. In the following two age groups, this moves on to flexible working. What is interesting about this progression is that in their younger years, when they are most concerned about fair pay, the gender pay gap is at its smallest at any stage of their lives. It is in women's mid-careers when the gender pay gap increases, coinciding with the time when many women have children.

When it comes to the work environment, there is a strong sense among all women that reality falls well short of expectation when it comes to fair pay and support from leadership and management. The awareness around the lack of equal gender rights is very evident. Women are also looking for network and mentor support to help them with career progression, but are finding it largely absent in the workplace. The areas that are seen as clear and available are return-to-work and maternity support and childcare provision. Organisations have therefore done a good job in making this an essential and understood provision for female employees.

BREAKING FREE OF THE 'UNENTITLED MINDSET'

At The Female Lead we have carried out deep research in several specific areas. One of these was named the 'Unentitled Mindset'. With this research, we wanted to find out what prevents women from progressing in their mid-careers and sees them moving to a significantly flatter career trajectory than men as they reach these years. We have always known that women do not need fixing and that women are smart, ambitious and passionate about finding fulfilment. So why is it that at a time in their lives when women consistently rate their work as their second most fulfilling pillar for two decades, do their average hourly wages plateau while men's average wages are still on an upwards trajectory (see Figure 10.2)?

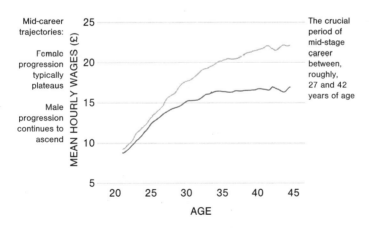

Figure 10.2. Mid-career trajectories.

Fundamentally, we wanted to understand the driving forces behind the persistent inequalities in gender pay and career progression. Firstly, our research highlighted where progress had been made so we could lay some of the myths around women and work to rest and, secondly, it demonstrated where the sticking points still are, as these require everyone's focus. This was done by comparing our current research with the results from a similar study in 1994 by the same researcher, psychologist Terri Apter. We then wrapped this up by discussing some of the ways forward that would help close this gap.

OUTDATED PRESUMPTIONS

Let's begin with the outdated presumptions. These are the myths surrounding who women are, the kinds of bias they are likely to face and what they want from work. We begin with these so that they can be put aside, and we can then focus on the real concerns that women are facing. Our research highlighted five fundamental outdated presumptions:

1. **Women resist the term 'ambitious' and suffer inner conflict about being career-focused.**
   What our research actually showed was that all of the participants were ambitious and embraced this with pride. They valued their independence and were dedicated to useful, high-impact and challenging work. These results contrasted with what was found in the 1994 study, in which women felt conflicted about ambition, competition, career identity and independence.

2. **Motherhood trumps all else and shifts career and professional identity to the back seat.**

All the women interviewed told us their career was fundamental to their sense of self and purpose. This included both women who were mothers and those who weren't.

3. **Women are uncomfortable earning more than their partners and place less value on their earning power.**
   All of the participants put a high value on financial independence. They equated this with personal power, the power to claim equality in a relationship and the power to leave an uncomfortable relationship. Job satisfaction was still more highly rated than increased income, but the respondents wanted to be paid fairly and equally.

4. **Imposter syndrome is a significant inhibitor to job performance and drive.**
   Among the respondents, 26% described a time when they had felt imposter syndrome but they were not deterred by it. Instead, they embraced a capability mindset and worked through it by seeing it as a challenge to work to their strengths and learn new skills.

5. **That female workers (particularly mothers) are more averse to embracing new challenges and risks.**
   Changing jobs was always seen as daunting, but the participants' willingness to do this was linked to their desire for satisfying work conditions. Satisfaction with their work was generally related to it being challenging, feeling comfortable in the workplace and having the opportunity to make a positive impact and grow.

PERSISTENT PROBLEMS

Importantly, our research also highlighted five areas where there were persistent sticking areas that continued to restrict women's progress. All of these areas were linked by one common theme – what we have called the 'Unentitled Mindset'.

1. **An Unentitled Mindset persists at the pay negotiation table.**
   One example of this internalised bias is a lack of confidence in negotiating pay increases and promotions. The workplace experience leaves participants unsure of their entitlement to promotion, more family friendly conditions or increased pay. When they did make these requests, they spent significant energy ensuring their case was watertight and reported being unsure of the rules for negotiation.

   Our research has shown that the two most significant gaps in terms of fulfilment in the workplace are fair pay, and promotion and career development (see Figure 10.3).

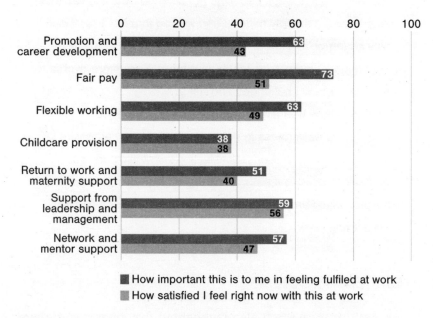

■ How important this is to me in feeling fulfiled at work
■ How satisfied I feel right now with this at work

Figure 10.3. Career development fulfiment gaps in the workplace.

2. Intersectionality offers fewer escape routes from persistent bias. The 1994 study showed that the participants believed that overt gender bias was something they had to live with. Our current research shows the participants resisted overt bias and would challenge it whenever it occurred. However, overt bias was intensified when it was combined with a bias towards race, ethnicity, disability, sexuality or religion. There were fewer escape routes from bias, particularly because calling it out was often more difficult.

Figure 10.4 shows that female ethnic minorities feel disconnected at work and have low satisfaction in the areas of enjoyment, satisfaction and power.

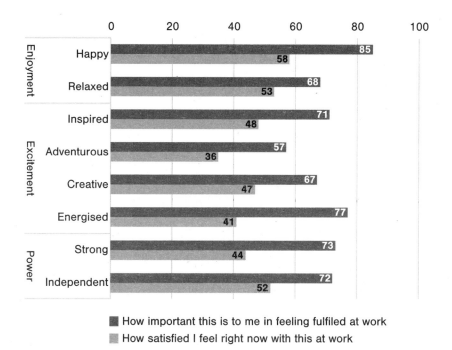

■ How important this is to me in feeling fulfiled at work
■ How satisfied I feel right now with this at work

Figure 10.4. Fulfilment gaps in the workplace for ethnic minority women.

3. Persistent bias towards mothers returning from maternity leave.

Participants reported that overall bias towards women in most workplaces was reducing and that, in many cases, it was manageable or on the margins of women's working lives. However, there was one type of bias that continues to endanger career progression, which was expectation bias directed towards women returning from maternity leave. This contributed to the Unentitled Mindset. This bias led to lower expectations of these women's contributions, commitment and ability to take on responsibilities and challenges. Participants who had experienced or witnessed it saw this as a significant impediment to career progression. This issue was further exacerbated by a lack of visible senior mothers 'making it work', which had a disabling effect on younger childless females, pregnant women and recent returners.

Our research has shown that working women have low satisfaction when it comes to their return to work and maternity support (see Figure 10.5).

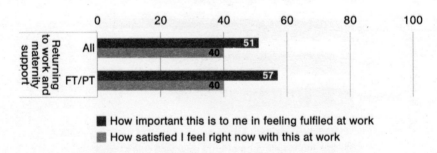

■ How important this is to me in feeling fulfiled at work
■ How satisfied I feel right now with this at work

Figure 10.5. Maternity support fulfilment gaps in the workplace.

4. A 'flexibility penalty' exists for part-time work and full-time workers with a degree of freedom around their schedule. Participants observed that even full-time work, when done flexibly, incurs a career penalty and contributes to the entitlement gap. This applies even when the flexibility is minimal and only means they don't have to work overtime. All types of flexible working, including part-time, time-shifted, compressed hours or the option to work remotely positions the women who do it as 'less than' other employees. Furthermore, participants reported that this flexibility penalty would last longer than the period in which they used it, therefore having a long-reaching impact on women's careers.

Figure 10.6 shows that women are not satisfied with flexible working, especially leaders or managers.

5. The burden of the 'mental load'.

Even where household chores and childcare were relatively evenly split in a relationship, the mental load still fell to the woman in the vast majority of cases. This mental load included the complex daily organisation of all caring and household

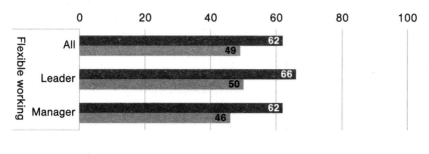

■ How important this is to me in feeling fulfiled at work
■ How satisfied I feel right now with this at work

Figure 10.6. Flexible working fulfilment gaps in the workplace.

179

responsibilities when parents were at work. This was a huge issue in the 1994 study and although there has been a significant improvement in men's contributions and their expectations of partnership and fatherhood, most of the participating women reported that far more childcare tasks fell to them. Several women without children cited this as a contributing reason for why they had chosen not to have children.

Our research has shown that women in a relationship and with children are more likely to be solely responsible for financial planning and control (See Figure 10.7).

The overall outcome of this research is that women have been socially conditioned to feel less entitled than men in all areas of their life, which creates an entitlement gap. This Unentitled Mindset is a persistent problem women face in their careers. It is a toxic internalised bias that leads to women lacking confidence at work, particularly when negotiating pay rises, or asking for promotions or flexible working. Many women in the study described

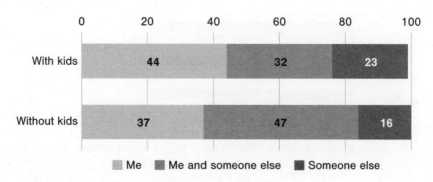

Figure 10.7. Who is responsible for financial planning/control.

being unsure whether they deserved better conditions. This stemmed from knowing they were worth more in terms of pay and flexibility but still being unsure of their claim to it.

This Unentitled Mindset can be seen in all areas of women's lives, not just the workplace. It is insidious because if women expect less, they will not complain about having less. Even though it is called a *mindset*, we are not suggesting that the problem lies entirely within women's heads and can be simply resolved by women changing the way they think. Instead, it is firmly part of the way that society conditions women to expect less. It is a learned behaviour from years of social conditioning to take up less space and quietly remain on the sidelines.

Closing this entitlement gap needs us to approach it in two ways. First, we need to address the embedded structures in society and the workplace that prevent women from accessing equal entitlements. Dr Terri Apter, who conducted the research, recommends that businesses do the following:

1. Highlight positive policies

   Women's experience teaches them, for example, that flexibility is rare, and that if offered, then asking for more – such as higher pay or status or responsibility – would risk their employer's good will, and possibly even their job. To change the environment, organisations simply need to make their willingness to embrace flexibility salient.

2. Proactively invite pay discussions

   Organisations need to understand how the environment (as opposed to the attitude of anyone in the organisation) triggers the 'Unentitled Mindset', but they can correct it. Inviting pay discussions, clarifying the possible outcomes, explaining how and when and with whom these discussions should be held, goes a long way towards reducing the ambiguity in which women are more likely to experience an 'Unentitled Mindset'.

The second way of closing the entitlement gap is promoting greater self-awareness and removing internal barriers to women developing a healthy sense of their entitlement. When it comes to negotiating pay rises and promotions, training and development are needed for both the employer and employee so that they can understand the change and context in which promotion and pay rises are discussed.

In a recent poll on LinkedIn, we asked our audience, 'Do you ever find it hard to speak up in meetings?' We received 44,557 votes, and the responses were:

- Yes: 56%
- No: 43%
- Other: 1%

Tips: How to ask for a pay rise

Fifteen per cent of men reported their salary negotiations resulted in more money compared to only four per cent of women. In response to this, I've created a five-step strategy to help women negotiate better pay rises:

Step 1: Earn it first, ask second

Before asking for a pay rise, you should be able to prove that you are dedicated and valuable to the company you work for. Managers and owners reward people who they trust and who are effective. There are a few ways you can do this:

- Start a side project
- Help colleagues
- Take on extra responsibilities
- Exceed expectations
- Keep track of your achievements

Step 2: Know your worth

Think of yourself as a business. Draw up a case for yourself and sell yourself based on your personal branding. Answer these questions in your business case:

- What have you generated?
- Why do they need you?
- What are the numbers?
- How can you become irreplaceable?

Step 3: Be a savvy negotiator

Savvy negotiation means coming to a pay-rise meeting with all the facts at hand and being clear about what you want and why you deserve it. Pay attention to the language you use and also your body language. For example, instead of saying, 'I'm looking for around £5,000', say, 'My proposal is £5,000, and here's why.'

Being a savvy negotiator includes:

- Researching the market
- Establishing the facts
- Asking outright for a pay rise

Step 4: Don't make it personal

Begin your case ambitiously but credibly. Make sure you use confident language but don't make it personal. If you start to hear some refusals, you can respond to them in the following ways:

If they say, 'This is a lot more than we have budgeted for this role', respond with, 'I understand. I also believe I bring more to the table than your average employee. For example ...'

If they say, 'Unfortunately, we can only go as high as ...' respond with, 'I understand. I'd like to set up a timeline to revisit the terms again in X months.'

If it gets heated, respond collaboratively rather than confrontationally, such as, 'I am confident we can get to a place we both feel good about'.

Step 5: Persevere

If it doesn't go to plan, don't just give up. It might not happen the first time, but that doesn't mean it won't happen next time. Find strength in the setback and persevere by setting deadlines and objectives for the next meeting. How you respond to a refusal defines you as a negotiator, and remember to always end a conversation politely.

Karen Blackett, CEO of GroupM UK and Country Manager of WPP UK

My advice to anyone starting out is to network. It sounds like a grubby word, perhaps something to do with going to pubs and restaurants, which is no use if you don't drink or don't have the time, capacity or availability. But networking can be all sorts of things: going to a training programme, or an event, or talking to people on social media. If you have an opportunity, always try to say yes, because you never know who you might meet. Some of my cheerleaders, the people who help me through and encourage me when imposter syndrome hits, are people I've met that way.

In the past, the most senior, global roles in my industry have gone to men who could travel two weeks a month. The pandemic has shown us other possible ways of working. I was very clear, when I said I was pregnant, that I was as ambitious as ever, that I intended to be even more productive, but that I was going to work in a different way. I was promoted 11 months after having a child, and I was a single mum. I had the support of a boss who saw what I was capable of. To this day, I don't think he realises that I'm a woman and I'm black. He just saw talent.

THE HIDDEN RISKS OF HYBRID WORKING

The Covid-19 pandemic led to an acceleration of most office-based workers adopting hybrid work patterns for this period. Large swathes of the workforce were told to work from home, which transformed the long-term availability of flexible working. Hybrid working has long been seen as a potential game-changer for women and underrepresented groups in the workforce, but it is also a relatively new concept to be adopted on such a large scale.

From our previous research, we knew that women generally love the idea of hybrid working as it allows them to multitask. However, business leaders and researchers have already highlighted potential pitfalls for women. The Female Lead wanted to fully explore the lived experience of hybrid working, how both women and men experience it and what they might need to do to manage their careers if adopting a hybrid work pattern. Therefore, we interviewed an equal split of female and male hybrid workers from various sectors and seniority to conduct this research. What we discovered was that there are several benefits of hybrid working, but also some hidden risks as well. The rewards of hybrid working for women and men are:

- Workers feel trusted and respected as they have greater control over their schedules and work arrangements.
- Workers are able to adjust their working style and environment to improve personal productivity.
- Enhanced flexibility allows hybrid workers to focus on their health and wellbeing.
- Workers report reduced costs for travel and childcare and less time spent on their commute.
- The flexibility of hybrid working is a game-changer for those with caring responsibilities.

As the above shows, the rewards that come from hybrid working can benefit both the employer and the employee. They allow the employee to have a more balanced approach to their work, including focusing on their health and wellbeing, and being able to manage their caring responsibilities while also adjusting their working style and environment to increase their productivity.

However, our research also highlighted four key areas where hybrid working causes a negative impact, particularly the career experiences of women:

- **Invisible workers.** Women double down on tasks and will work longer hours or work when ill to avoid stereotypes about hybrid workers. However, working behind a digital wall means this additional work might not be visible and might go unnoticed and unrecognised.
- **Shielded from office politics.** Women are shielded from political interactions, which risks them feeling left out of the loop and lacking the networks they need to leverage career support.
- **Slowing progression.** The risks of hybrid working combined with a lack of learning opportunities and less flexibility in senior roles place women in danger of slower career progression.
- **Loss of joy and purpose.** Women miss the camaraderie with colleagues. When this is combined with increased isolation and video fatigue, many found their roles joyless and struggled to find meaning in their work.

This was ground-breaking research because, on the surface, hybrid working is one of the possible solutions for women juggling caring roles with work. However, it would appear from the data that women are exchanging increased work for a lower profile and connectivity. The solution to this is not to send everyone back to the office full-time. Instead, organisations need to find ways to make hybrid working more inclusive through policies and procedures. As a result of this research, we created an expert advisory board to provide practical recommendations and solutions for organisations in the form of a toolkit to enhance inclusivity for the four areas:

1. Invisible workers

- Reframe and communicate what 'productivity' is all about.
- Managers to champion employees upwards and sideways.
- Find ways to showcase employees without relying on managers.
- Support employees to separate work from home.

2. Shielded from office politics

- Reframe 'politics' to encourage inclusive interaction.
- Create transparent communities.
- Incentivise (not mandate) the office.

3. Slowing progression

- Onboard employees in-person.
- Provide regular shadowing opportunities.
- Design flexibility into all roles.
- Provide sponsorship.

4. Loss of joy and purpose

- Invest in purposeful team bonding.
- Encourage camaraderie via transparent online social groups.
- Create a vibrant office environment.

Fundamentally, women in hybrid work need to be seen and commended for their efforts and have equal access to and flexibility for job opportunities as people working in the office full-time. The outcome, if this is achieved, is that at a time in their lives when work is incredibly important to women but they are often juggling other responsibilities as well, they will still find joy and satisfaction in their work.

When we interviewed Vanessa Kingori OBE, Publishing Director of British *Vogue*, she observed that: 'There's a whole generation of women who have downplayed the fact that they're mothers in order to excel, so this is why there's no template.' She told us what she was going to about it.

I'm going to make my life a lot easier, and, perhaps women coming through who want to have both a career and a family at the same time, I'm going to try and make it a little easier for them, by showing I am a mother, that I am doing all the things that mothers do, but I'm also doing a good job. I think that's really important and I would love to see even more of it from other women, it all helps us cheer each other along.'

Much has changed in the world of work for women, and it will continue to change. Many more women are now self-employed than they used to be, and this trend is set to continue. Morag Ross, a freelance award-winning make-up artist, told us that she gets satisfaction from collaborating with other creative minds towards a great final goal and that she loves the travel. She went on to say that the hours can be gruelling, so she has to have stamina and commitment. Also in film, because there is a lot of money invested, there is pressure to deliver every day. She observed that when you are self-employed it is important to love what you do. If you are going to follow your dream and possibly live in a precarious way, you need a certain amount of passion for it and have support from the people around you.

The Academy Award-winning costume designer, Sandy Powell, has had a similar experience of being self-employed and the passion required to fuel it. She told us that being a costume designer is not an easy job.

> When you are working, you have to be completely and utterly dedicated and prepared to give up the rest of your life for the duration. If you didn't have a passion for it, it would be arduous. I hope to carry on enjoying my work as much as I do. If something doesn't inspire me, I won't do it, and there have been one or two jobs that I've started and then recognised that I am not excited and pulled out. However much I might need the money, I would rather scrape by for a bit until I'm doing something that I really like.

Bobbi Brown's advice for women who are thinking of starting their own business is to:

> Stop thinking and start doing. Even if it's not something that you're going to be able to complete right away, just start. Set your alarm an hour earlier. Do it on a weekend. That's how you become successful: once you start, you just keep doing it.

Nell Merlino, who is the creator of Take Our Daughters to Work Day, worked on The Female Lead in London with me for a short while. When we interviewed her, she told us that she believes that digital natives have an opportunity to shape the world as we can now quantify our lives, and all the work we do, including unpaid, at home. She feels this gives us the opportunity to say, 'This is what we contribute to the economy, and this is where we want to take it.' She sees the importance of this data and goes on to say that we never had the numbers before, and if we want to be driving the bus, these are the numbers we need.

The changes in the world of work for women are set to continue. The ONS has confirmed that 18% of women do not have children by the time they reach 45 years old.[5] This number is also likely to grow as, for the first time, half of women who have recently reached 30 years old have not had children. We often talk about the caring responsibilities of women with children but, with an ageing population, women without children can often find themselves caring for their elderly parents or relatives.

Women who don't have children are also judged as harshly as women with children in the workplace. Often women find that when they reach their thirties, there may be an anticipation that they will have children shortly, so they potentially miss out on promotions or challenging internal assignments.

All of this contributes to women earning, and therefore having, less money than men. This economic gap has a huge impact on women's current situations and their future. Because the gender pay gap is just the start of how much less money women have than men. The gender *money* gap is much wider, and its long-term effects can be devastating for women's equality.

Brenda Berkman, first NYC female firefighter

I was a law student, married, living in New York and working on cases with my father-in-law's firm. We represented women police officers who were suing the police for discrimination, and we were handling a case for the New York City firefighters. At that time women couldn't even apply. All the firefighters I knew loved their jobs, which you certainly can't say about lawyers.

I've always wanted to help people and that's what the fire department does – when people are at their most desperate, they call us. It doesn't matter if the call comes in the middle of the night, in a tsunami, or from a poor neighbourhood where no one speaks English – the firefighters go. So when the law changed to force the fire department to open its doors to women, I applied . . .

When I turned up to take the written exam, the men were quite hostile. It's hard to perform when people think you're a nut. I'd always played sports, I'd run marathons and I worked out. I trained for the physical examination like crazy, carrying my husband up and down the stairs, running, chopping wood.

It was clear to me that my score wasn't being kept properly. They weren't crediting me. The exam had been changed and wasn't measuring actual physical abilities. Not one of the 90 women who showed up to take it passed. I thought there had to be one woman in New York who was capable of being a firefighter. So I talked to Bella Azbug [the leading feminist activist] and to a lawyer at NYU, my law school, and we went to see the man who was in charge of examination for the fire department. He laughed in our faces.

So I decided to file a lawsuit. That entailed testifying under oath that if I won I would quit practising the law and take the job; otherwise the case would have been thrown out. Five years after I took the exam, we proved that it was not job-related and about 40 of us entered the fire department's academy.

CHAPTER 11

MONEY

Much has been said about the gender pay gap, including publicity and campaigning around the subject. However, the gender *money* gap should receive as much attention, if not more. This is because the gender pay gap is just the tip of the iceberg. Alongside a lower hourly wage, women are also less likely to be employed than men and have fewer working hours than men, resulting in a huge earnings reduction. Research by the Institute of Fiscal Studies has shown that as recently as 2019, the average working-age woman in the UK earned 40% less than her male counterpart.[1] This massive gap in earnings leaves women with less disposable money and potentially reliant on others for financial support. It also cements the Unentitled Mindset discussed in Chapter 10, causing women to have smaller pensions, and fewer assets and investments. Fundamentally, in a society where money equals power, women end up with less of both.

When we interviewed Nell Merlino, creator of Take Our Daughters to Work Day, she explained why it is so important that women have their own money.

I started out as a union organiser, helping women to get a better wage, so I was aware from the beginning of this need to have enough money so you are not dependent on anyone else. It became clear to me that the greatest opportunity for that kind of freedom was owning your own business. Starting in business makes it possible to live the life you want to lead. I am not interested in money for the sake of money – I am interested in freedom.

Although there is some overlap with the Work pillar, when we talk about the Money pillar this includes:

- Personal finances
- Pensions
- The money gap
- Unpaid work

Ann Cairns, Executive Vice-Chair at Mastercard, who I have known for many years and is a delight to work with, explained to us that financial independence is key to women's freedom. She went on to say that when we have the ability to earn a decent wage, to own and protect our property, we have choices.

Inequality in financial positions also threatens women's ability to focus on what fulfils them. When people's basic needs are not met, they naturally turn their attention towards the fundamentals of living. One area that can require a great deal of their focus is housing. In England, the average rent takes 43% of the average woman's earnings, compared to 28% of the average man's. Trying to secure low-cost rental properties is time-consuming and stressful and means that women have less opportunity to live by themselves than men and therefore have to live in shared accommodation.

Women also live longer than men while earning less, so they are 'under-pensioned' and underinvested. With an ageing population to consider, we are already in the middle of a time when women often experience poverty in their retirement years – a situation that is only likely to get worse. If women earn less than men throughout their lifetimes, they are less likely to be able to pay into a private pension and fewer, or no, working hours affect their state pension as well. When women are unable to be financially independent in their later years, they have to rely on overstretched state provisions or family and friends for care, which disproportionately affects women from poorer backgrounds. A recent increase in the pension age in the UK from age 65 to 66 saw a rise of 9% of women and 7% of men staying in paid work at 65 years old.[2] This increase hit the country's most deprived areas in particular, where these percentages have seen a rise to 13% for women and 10% for men.

This disparity in economic wealth between men and women stretches throughout society. Women with lower earnings do more unpaid work within the household, and women with highly lucrative roles at the top of S&P 500 companies (the 500 largest publicly traded companies in the USA) only control around 1% of the shares among fellow leaders.[3]

In addition, no one ever talks about the downside of suddenly receiving a big cheque. Of course not. Who wouldn't want that to happen? Just imagine the fun of spending it! Money gives you choices and freedom but it also brings responsibilities and many decisions to make. If, like me, you didn't grow up with wealth, by the time you hit your target and cash in, you often don't have the knowledge or financial planning in place. You've spent so long worrying about your business growth that you never consider what might happen when you stop and the tables turn.

You wake up one day and realise you've made it financially and will get a big payout, but when that large cheque arrives, everyone suddenly appears. We wouldn't have gone public with the sale of our business, but we had no choice as the transaction was published in Tesco's accounts. Suddenly there was financial planning, investment 'opportunities' and invitations onto boards and charitable foundations. The most casual of conversations could turn into an investment pitch for a new venture. It happened over and over again. We became attuned to the clues and would think, *Please don't do this. We were just having a conversation about the Congestion Charge, and now you're asking me for money.*

The money my husband and I made was hard won over many years. We had risked our careers and savings throughout. We didn't inherit it, so it took us a long time to become accustomed to this new situation and how some people's attitudes changed towards us. You have to build confidence around money and learn what you want to do with it rather than listening to people telling you what you should do with it. It's another journey with so many twists and turns.

Tips: Handling money

I am not a money expert, but I know a woman that is. Tiffany Aliche is an author and financial advisor who has spoken before for The Female Lead. Her advice is to 'Get Good with Money'. Here are some of her tips:

Advice from Tiffany Aliche

Research shows that women make 70% of the financial choices in their household. If a woman doesn't understand money, this has a huge impact on the finances of most households. Mastering your money is therefore critical to a happier life. Women who do understand money and how to manage it also pass it on and help their partner, their family and friends. Money can be simple maths:

Budgeting and saving = getting out of debt

Wills or trusts = protection and peace of mind

Women are capable but are constantly told that they are 'no good' at money or 'don't care'. Money is not just about power. It's about freedom, as it gives you options, increases positivity and abundance.

When money management goes wrong, it damages lives. It can mean not having a safe environment to grow up in, and here fear and shame creep in. Shame makes you feel bad about yourself and can keep you in a dark place. Evidence suggests that money problems can also be isolating. You feel you're alone and you don't speak out for shame. It can be bad for your mental and physical health.

But you are not alone. Struggling with personal finances is common. It is not a condemnation of your character. Give yourself the grace and space to learn to welcome in options and solutions.

To 'Get Good With Money', think about these ten aspects of your finances to live your greatest and richest life:

1. Budget-building
2. Saving (like a squirrel)
3. Debt (digging out of debt)
4. Credit (scoring high)

5. Learning how to earn (increase income)

6. Learning how to invest (invest like an insider)

7. Insurance (getting good with it)

8. Net worth (growing rich-ish through earning more than you spend)

9. Finance professionals/your team

10. Estate-planning (leaving a legacy; i.e. your bank account, your funeral, etc.)

HOW THE IMPORTANCE OF MONEY CHANGES AS WE AGE

Money is the fifth most important area, on average, to women's overall fulfilment throughout their lifetime. The importance of this area gradually grows throughout women's 20s and early 30s before peaking at age 35–44 (see Figure 11.1). It then steadily declines as women get older and potentially become more financially stable.

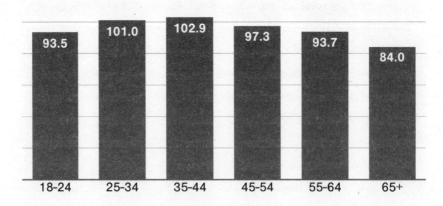

Figure 11.1. Relative importance of money.

For all age groups, Money is far less important than Work as a key pillar. However, while Money overall is less of a concern, financial security raises an alarm for women and shows that they have a high degree of dissatisfaction between what they desire and expect and what they actually get.

Work and Money are most important to women aged 35–44 as they build on their careers and finances, and this is the only age group for whom money is of great importance. Money is a much lower priority for the over 65s but as we will see, they are very concerned about financial security.

Money is a much more important area to personas such as Crisis Manager and Influencers and much less important to Bon Vivants, Everyone's Friend and Entertainers.

Roya Mahboob, technology entrepreneur and cofounder of Digital Citizen Fund
In 2010 I started Afghan Citadel Software Company with the aim of providing job opportunities for females. I also established IT centres – 11 located in schools – and we have educated almost 8,000 women and girls. Men in conservative societies often don't see women as first-class citizens, but connectivity enables a woman to earn money, which can give her more status in the family. Once such woman had been a student until she married and had children. Then she had the responsibility of the home, and her husband wouldn't pay for her university studies. She began writing articles for the Women's Annex Foundation and got paid well in bitcoin. She bought a laptop and started a successful fashion business, which has made her very popular with her husband!

> My mum was my greatest influence because she did not rely on my father. When they moved to Iran, she couldn't work, so she started making handicrafts, just to be independent.

HOW THE IMPORTANCE OF MONEY CHANGES DEPENDING ON OUR PERSONAL CIRCUMSTANCES

Three responses show money as the most important area of fulfilment. The first is for women who are ethnic minorities in the country where they live. For these women, money is slightly more important than other areas of their lives. However, compared to women who are part of the ethnic majority of the country where they live, it is much more important. The emotional driver behind this is that many women who are part of the ethnic minority in the country where they live place a high amount of importance on feeling in control about being fulfilled, much more so than women who are in the majority.

Second is women who earn their own money but live in a house with shared occupancy, as they have to stand on their own two feet and pay their way. Again, they only see money as slightly more important to the other areas of their lives. This group of women also place a great deal of importance on feelings of excitement and enjoyment, and significantly more so than other groups of women. Third, and finally, money is considered more important to women who don't use social media, perhaps because they are busy working and don't have the time to surf or scroll the internet. For these women, the feeling of control is most important.

Money is the least important pillar for women who are married and for women who use social media. It is also the least important area for breadwinners who, like married women, consider their relationships the most fulfilling area of their life. This is perhaps because women who work often worry about what they have given up in their personal life and thus prioritise relationships so they don't fall short of expectations at home and with the family.

*　　*　　*

The responses on money are distinctive, but they are not as volatile as the Health pillar. Geographically, Money is much more important to women in the USA and India than in other countries. These results clearly reflect how much money is talked about and celebrated there. America is famously the country where anyone can arrive poor and become a millionaire. It is a culture that celebrates wealth-building and entrepreneurial skills, even though this clearly leans more towards men than women when considering the leading billionaires over there, such as Elon Musk, Bill Gates and Jeff Bezos. In a much poorer country, like India, money understandably tends to trump issues like Relationships.

THE TOPICS OF MOST IMPORTANCE WITHIN THE MONEY PILLAR BY AGE GROUP

Women start by being most worried about their future earning potential. In the next age group, their attention turns to living within their means and building investments for the future. The topics that most women focus on in their younger years within the

Money pillar show that women are aware of the importance of having money in the future. Women then focus on their salary, and this is when the gender pay gap increases. Women aged 45–54 are most focused on economic independence, which also coincides with a time just after the most common age for women to divorce. Towards the end of their lives, women focus on their investments as a critical source of income. The key takeaways for each age group are:

AGE 18–24

- Money is dominated by salary, and it is in this group that one of the largest differences between expectations and current situation occurs.
- This is counteracted by a strong belief in future earning capabilities for this group of women.

AGE 25–34

- Women in this group are fairly typical for the overall patterns regarding money concerns. They are slightly more confident about living within their means, but otherwise show little variation to patterns overall.

AGE 35–44

- At this stage in their lives, many women place a higher amount of importance on their salary.
- They are also quite close to the average results for women in relation to money overall.

AGE 45-54

- In terms of money, economic independence becomes important to many women at this stage of their lives.
- They also show an increased concern around their ability to manage debt, perhaps as the costs of older children start to appear and possibly affect their lifestyle.

AGE 55-64

- Building investments for the future becomes the most important area in terms of money to these women.

AGE 65 AND OVER

- Women at this stage care about living within their means and they don't feel satisfied making financial savings.
- The results also show a marked sense of lack of financial security which is much more pronounced at this age, possibly as divorce, retirement or lower incomes become more of a reality for this group of women.

Overall, women definitely do not feel satisfied with their financial security. They also seem more than aware that their salaries are well below those of their male colleagues and find this less than acceptable. Making savings and building investments for the future are areas that fall short of what women want to see and the safety and security they aspire to. From the scores received, we can see that much of women's focus is about living within their means and having manageable debt.

Another factor that influences the amount of money women have is the amount of unpaid work they do compared to men. This includes household responsibilities and caring for older and younger relatives. If women spend longer on these unpaid tasks, this leads to less time for paid work and, consequently, less money.

Our research on the Unentitled Mindset highlighted that in 1974–75 women did 31.7 hours of unpaid work each week, and by 2014–15 this had only reduced to 29 hours (see Figure 11.2). Compared to 1975, women do fewer unpaid hours but still nearly

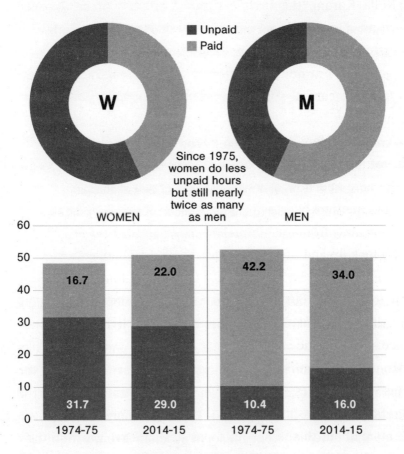

Figure 11.2. Paid vs. unpaid hours per week.

twice as many as men, who have increased their unpaid work from 10.4 hours to 16. What is also clear is how much less paid work women do compared to men: 22 hours compared to 34 hours. It is this reduction in paid hours, as well as the gender pay gap, that is the main contributor to the gender money gap.

Whether money is high on your fulfilment list or not, it often provides freedom of choice, allowing you to decide your future rather than having it dictated to you by your circumstances. We need what money gives us, which is power, options and freedom. As Rolla Karam, the Interim Chief Content Officer at Orbit Showtime Network, said when we interviewed her, 'I always understood the value of money. It's important to me to work and get paid. I'm not saying money is everything, but it means you can take care of your family. You can be independent. You can help.'

We are therefore not helping ourselves by ignoring the importance of money. Quite often women will find themselves focused on the here and now, when they are worrying about the housekeeping, the weekly or daily shop or carer costs. This takes their attention away from the future. One day, later in our lives, many of us will look up and find we're underinvested and under-pensioned, and even if we have a windfall such as an inheritance, we're more likely to give it to our dependants rather than keep it for our old age. All of this makes women vulnerable and victims of circumstance and altruistic choices.

Money also significantly influences the trajectory of governments and societies, and when women don't hold as much as men, they have less chance of swaying this influence. Before we talk more about this in the third part of the book, we will finish with the last pillar of fulfilment, which is Society.

Joyce Banda, President of Malawi from 7 April 2012 to 31 May 2014

I was married at age 21. By age 26, I had three children. I was in an abusive marriage for 10 years. I realised that if I wanted a better life for my three children I needed to make a move. At the time, there was so much pressure to remain married, but I moved out, and went and studied again. I realised that the economic empowerment of women is key. When you are economically empowered, you can provide better nutrition, health and education for your children. By 1985, not only had I married again, but I had grown my business to a level where I was able to make a contribution to the household. When you make a financial contribution, you gain respect.

In 1990, now that I was – by Malawi standards – a rich woman, I looked at all those who were not as fortunate as myself and I decided to start an organisation called the National Association of Business Women. By 1997, that organisation was the largest rural network for women in Malawi and 50,000 women had been empowered. I received the Africa Prize for Leadership for the Sustainable End of Hunger, and I looked at what I could do with the $50,000 that I received as the award money.

I decided my contribution would be to send as many girls as possible to school. I had promised myself this when I was 14 and Chrissie didn't go to school. So I started the Joyce Banda Foundation. The first day, there were only three girls, and now, the Joyce Banda Foundation has sent 6,500 girls to school, and 1,500 to university.

CHAPTER 12

SOCIETY

When I was in my twenties and thirties, the business world (actually, the world in general) was not as politically correct as it is today. It was most certainly a man's world and women were not always taken that seriously. That behaviour was rife no matter how high up the corporate ladder I got and also into my time as the CEO of my company. I will never forget a conversation I ended up having in the basement of an office with an executive from a huge retailer. He was frustrated as I wouldn't agree to his terms for a joint venture. We were using an analogy of a joint venture being like a marriage. He was getting closer and closer to me and kept repeating that there had to be trust in a marriage. I couldn't agree to his terms because they would have made the deal totally unprofitable. This frustrated him. At that moment, he pressed right up to my face and said, 'In a marriage, I want a wife, not a whore.' It stunned me and left me shocked and undermined. I still think about that conversation today and how a woman would never speak to a man like that. That conversation might still happen today, which is one of the many ways that I know gender equality hasn't been attained.

The Society pillar of fulfilment starts with gender inequality but encompasses the many areas it affects. It includes female representation, ethnic discrimination and social equality, to name a few. Many of the Female Leads we have interviewed have contributed in various ways to societal issues. It seems a common thread that they give back in one way or another, whether it's devoting their lives to campaigning for justice, mentoring others or setting up non-profits later on in their careers. The common thread is that they want to contribute to making this world a better place for future generations. The Society pillar therefore includes:

- Gender equality
- Female representation
- Ethnic discrimination
- Social equality
- Environment
- Social media

Before diving into our own data research on this pillar, I want to share one key element that stands out from our research about fulfilment: women who are the most fulfilled are more likely to care about society. The interesting question is whether this is cause or effect. Is it that people who care about others are more fulfilled? Or is it that when we're fulfilled and happy in our own lives, we have more time and capacity to care for a larger section of society? Or a combination of both? Whatever the answer, it shows that the benefits of fulfilment are, literally, widespread.

Gina Miller gave us some advice on the realities of being a social justice campaigner.

To any young woman, or anyone wanting to be a campaigner – you're going into battle. Take some time to really know yourself, your strengths and your weaknesses. If you know your weaknesses, somebody else can't criticise and tell you what they are. You just say, 'Yes, I know.' It deflates their argument. Find how you are strongest. And no campaign can be achieved or won on your own.

HOW THE IMPORTANCE OF SOCIETY CHANGES AS WE AGE

The Society pillar is the least important aspect of most women's fulfilment throughout their lifetime. Its importance is highest when women are young, and in the age range of 18-24. Society's importance then sharply declines as women reach the age of 25-44 before increasing again in the later stages of women's lives (see Figure 12.1). However, it doesn't quite reach the heights it reached in women's younger years.

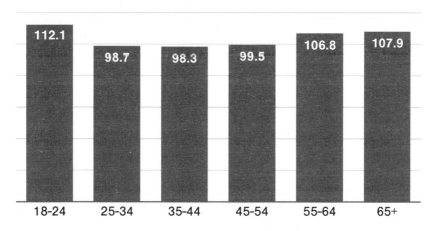

Figure 12.1. Relative importance of Society.

Even though Society is the least important area in women's fulfilment overall throughout their lifetime, it is still rated as the most prioritised for 18–24 year-olds who believe they can make a difference to the world and care about society more than any other age group.

The Society pillar is important to the Reformer persona, closely followed by the Achiever and Influencer personas.

HOW THE IMPORTANCE OF SOCIETY CHANGES DEPENDING ON OUR PERSONAL CIRCUMSTANCES

The Society pillar is held as the most important one by women who don't have children. This group also cares about society more than any of the other categories. Similarly, single women also rate Society as the most important area of their lives, compared to married or divorced women. They also place a lot of importance on feelings of power, and this is at a similar level to divorced women.

Women who are not breadwinners are significantly more likely to champion a cause or solve a problem. On average, the Society pillar is slightly more important to their fulfilment than other areas of their lives. Women who are not breadwinners place much more importance on feelings of enjoyment and feeling in control than feeling power. The last group who, on average, reports society as the most important pillar are women who use social media. The emotional driver behind this is the importance they place on the feeling of connectedness.

This last result is shown in reverse, where women who don't use social media generally rate Society as the least important pillar to them. Women with shared financial responsibility, on average, also see Society as the least important area.

When it comes to the importance of Society on a geographic basis, it is considered at the highest levels in Sweden, the Netherlands and Germany, whereas it is much lower in France and Switzerland. It is ranked extremely low in importance, relatively speaking, in India. Again, this reflects the more fundamental day-to-day problems women in the subcontinent face.

THE TOPICS OF MOST IMPORTANCE WITHIN THE SOCIETY PILLAR BY AGE GROUP

In Society, a key issue for women is gender equality, followed by environmentalism and social equality. The gap in what women expect and what they see today is extremely high in these three areas, especially gender equality. In fact, these are the three largest gaps we see in the survey. The top four or five gaps in what is expected and what women see are all to do with societal issues. This may, in part, be why Society appears to score so poorly in the survey because women perceive it to be the hardest area to impact, change and make progress in.

AGE 18–24

- When it comes to society, women of this age are most passionate about gender equality.
- They feel connected to society but need to feel much more in control.

AGE 25–34

- Improving social equality is important to these women, and they feel a gap in satisfaction when it comes to this.
- They don't feel powerful when it comes to this area of their lives.

AGE 35–44

- Many women place high importance on ending ethnic or religious discrimination at this stage of their lives.
- They feel a large gap in satisfaction when it comes to protecting the environment.

AGE 45–54

- Protecting the environment is most important to these women, perhaps driven by feeling a responsibility for the planet for their children.

AGE 55–64

- Many women of this age group feel a lack of satisfaction regarding female representation in the media.
- They also care more about ending ethnic or religious discrimination – more so than any other age group.
- Generally, they are satisfied with how their impact on society makes them feel, but like women of all ages, they do not feel in control.

AGE 65 AND OVER

- Women aged 65 or over consider that Society is important, but score low on all dimensions in terms of the gap between their expectations and reality. The only exception to that is when it comes to gender equality.
- They feel a large gap in satisfaction when it comes to this area, more so than any other age group.
- They also feel the most out of control when it comes to the way society, and their contribution to it, fulfils them emotionally.

Nadia Murad, Nobel Peace Prize Laureate and UNODC Goodwill Ambassador

My advocacy work is never about prizes or recognition. It has always been about my community's need for justice and support. Initially, I did not want to accept the Nobel Prize because I did not think it would help Yazidis return home or hold ISIS accountable. I worried the world would think the Yazidi struggle was over because I had been awarded this prize. In the end, I accepted it because I hoped the Nobel would help provide a larger platform for raising awareness and resources to help our cause. It helped me to launch Nadia's Initiative and many impactful projects on the ground in Sinjar.

I want people to understand that no one wants to become a refugee. It is incredibly difficult to leave everything you know behind, cross a border, and learn to live in a new place. It is also often the only option for people whose homes have become unlivable due to persecution, poverty, natural disasters and violence. We want to return to our homeland and our communities. We know that foreign countries are not eager to take in more refugees. That is why the sustainable solution to preserving my community and culture is to invest in local governance, security and basic services, so Yazidis can live in safety and dignity.

I want to see my community heal. It requires justice, reparations, security, democratic governance and investment in Sinjar. Perpetrators must be held accountable in courts of law for genocide and sexual violence. Survivors should be compensated for what they lost and empowered to build a brighter future. All of these steps take political will, which is why my advocacy work and the work of other survivors is so critical to ensuring the international community will not forget the plight of the Yazidis.

Like the other pillars, the topics women focus on within the Society pillar change as they age. In general, women care more about protecting the environment as they get older, and the gap in satisfaction in this area is largest at ages 65 and over. At age 18-24, women are most passionate about gender inequality and female representation in the media and their industries. The topic of female representation in the media then returns to a place of importance at age 55-64. This is potentially because it is at a time when women of their age become less visible in the media or have limited roles to play.

Although Society is rarely a lead factor in driving fulfilment across all age groups, awareness of social inequalities is very evident. There is a striking dissatisfaction with gender equality and the considerations that are about our long-term health and values for the world. Women also care about protecting the environment and sustainability. They are also dissatisfied with society's inability to deliver what is needed to improve social equality, which they believe falls far short of their expectations.

*   *   *

There is a crucial topic within the Society pillar that many of the Female Leads have spoken about when we interviewed them: the violence that some women suffer from men. A global database of studies published in *The Lancet* shows that 27% of women aged 15–49 had experienced physical or sexual intimate partner violence in their lifetime.[1] Many of the Female Leads we spoke to have devoted their lives to helping women in these situations and providing education and resources to those involved and the many lives it affects.

When we interviewed Gina Miller for our second book, *The Female Lead* (Volume II): *We Rise By Lifting Others*, she told us of her experience of domestic violence.

After years of being on my own, looking after my special-needs daughter and building a business, I was exhausted. Then into my life walked this man who promised to be a wonderful father and husband. What I didn't know was that, after our marriage, he would systematically try to break me. Again, I was at a point in my life where no one would believe me, because successful middle-class women don't suffer from things like that, and he was very much a Pillar of Society. After a few years of a very destruc-tive, violent relationship, I had nowhere to go but I knew I had to leave. For three weeks my daughter and I lived in the car. That's when I decided that nobody was ever going to try and silence me or break me again.

There cannot be true gender equality until women are safe in their homes, at their workplaces and on the streets. This is fundamental to any campaign around gender equality, and includes the intimidation, verbal abuse and control that many women suffer on a daily basis. If in the future there is no gender pay gap or money gap, but women still do not have control over their bodies and their physical and psychological safety, we have not yet achieved gender equality.

Luiza Trajano, Chair of Brazilian retailer Magazine Luiza, decided to make a change within her own company to help her female employees. She told us:

I knew that a woman was killed every two hours, but we always assume it only happens far away from us. That was until a 37-year-old employee, a manager from Campinas, was killed by her husband while their son slept in the next bedroom. The next day I created a hotline for women in my company. We created a committee with clear goals and our first was called 'Bursting the Bubble'. Nobody was talking about violence against women. The less you talk, the more women remain in silence, the more deaths occur. The hotline is so effective because the husbands get scared when they realise the company is protecting their wives. We receive reports from employees to the hotline and it's men who help us the most. We worked hard on this and asked them to help. When they see a woman coming to work with bruises, they call our hotline. I am impressed at how male employees have helped with the programme. We don't want Denise's death to be in vain.

Sônia Guajajara, indigenous activist, environmentalist and politician

In 2019 we organised the first march of indigenous women in Brazil. It was the first one in the world and we gathered almost 4,000 women. Women came up to me and said: 'I want to be a leader. I want to have a role in organisations. I want to be a senator.' So many women revealed this to me and now we have 44 women elected as councillors and vice mayors and even a mayor. The important thing is that we empower more and more women.

Indigenous rights are fundamental for the life of our planet. These rights ensure a balanced environment. The indigenous fight and environmental fight cannot be separated. It is a single fight because we are nature. For Brazil and for the world it is urgent to break with the current economic model based on large scale production, unrestrained mining and the use of rivers for power plants. It is a model that does not support itself. Studies now show what we have been saying for thousands of years: that nature is not infinite. Society must understand this.

Historically this environmental issue has been left aside in public debates and politics. Today the whole world can see how urgent this fight is. Indigenous people treat the land as a mother. That is why we care because for us it is Mother Earth. And a mother is taken care of, is protected, and not sold. The fight for Mother Earth is the mother of all fights.

DISRUPT YOUR FEED

In 2017, The Female Lead set out to research what types of social-media interactions result in positive and negative mental-health outcomes for teenage girls. The link between social media and adverse mental-health outcomes had been clear for some years, but what we wanted to do was to see if the participants could change this outcome into a positive one by 'disrupting their feed'. This was the first study to be done this way, as previous efforts to combat the negative impact of social media had focused largely on restricting the use of it.

Jade Thirlwall, singer-songwriter and member of Little Mix, spoke to us for, *The Female Lead* (Volume II): *We Rise By Lifting Others*, about the impact social media has had on her and her changing attitude towards it.

> I find it strange that people go on social media to say something negative and tag us – they want us to see it. I have turned my Instagram tags off and rarely go on Twitter: I've found that it's important for my mental wellbeing to not be on my phone too much. I have been guilty of typing my name into Twitter and looking for the worst someone can say about me, just to confirm the insecurity I was already feeling. That's toxic and, over the years, I have had to learn to stop. Stopping giving my energy to that negativity was the best thing I could have done.

A recent Female Lead poll showed:

- 94% of respondents felt that social-media platforms and/or Government should do more to protect young people from extreme or harmful content online .
- 84% have personally made a conscious effort to develop better/ healthier social-media habits.

What we also wanted to explore was the untapped potential of social media to enhance teen aspiration and promote positive mental health that impacted their offline lives as well. We created a simple intervention for the participants to trial: introducing new, diverse and positive female role models into their social-media feeds. The participants were encouraged to take the lead in their social-media use by actively searching out content that furthered their passions and aspirations. They did this by following the social-media accounts of the inspiring Female Leads from our books and films. We created a pledge to help social media users disrupt their feed:

1. Scroll with purpose
2. Challenge the algorithm
3. Take the lead in your own feed

The results were striking. They showed that girls who did this displayed different traits from most teenage girls in the UK. The following year, the psychologist Dr Terry Apter also showed there was a direct link between who you followed on social media and your self-belief.

Tips: How to Disrupt Your Feed (DYF)

Social-media sites use powerful algorithms with one sole purpose: to keep you on their site. They want to do this because the longer you spend on their site, the more advertising they can show you and the more money they can make. Their algorithms monitor what content keeps you on the site the longest and feed you more of this.

To disrupt your feed, follow new accounts that break away from what you usually look for. Follow people who make you feel better about yourself or inspire you rather than ones you negatively compare yourself to. The algorithm will adjust to display more of this type of content to you.

Distinguish between passive use of social media, where you are scrolling through content mindlessly, and actively searching for posts that feed your interests. This is important because passive scrolling is associated with more negative emotions.

You can also influence your feed by dismissing some threads or profiles by using the 'This doesn't interest me' option.

Elizabeth Nyamayaro, United Nations Special Advisor for the World Food Programme

In my twenties, I decided I was going to chase my dream to work for the United Nations (UN). I landed at Heathrow Airport with a small suitcase and £250. Anything that could go wrong went wrong. I didn't know anyone in the UK. I ran out of money. I nearly became homeless. I worked as a janitor. Eventually I managed to put myself through university.

My family is very proud that I didn't give up; but, in terms of the actual work, it's sort of expected. There's an African saying: 'To whom much is given, much is expected.' Core to our African cultures is the ancient philosophy of *ubuntu*, the idea that a person is only a person through other persons: we are all connected by our shared humanity. What impacts one of us will eventually impact all of us in various ways. If you exist as part of a community, it's up to you to play your part in uplifting those around you.

In 2014, I found myself with the incredible opportunity, as United Nations Senior Advisor on Gender Equality, to figure out a way to uplift half of the world's population: women and girls. For a very long time, men and other genders have been excluded from this conversation. I immediately knew that we had to bring everyone together, including men. With the support of my colleagues, we created the HeForShe movement. Within three days, at least one man in every single country had joined; and within the first five days there were 1.2 billion online conversations.

HeForShe began to normalise the idea that gender inequality is society's issue, because when women gain, societies gain.

HeForShe gave men an opportunity to examine their privilege and say, 'I will not rape a woman,' rather than putting the burden on women not to get raped; 'I will not marry a child,' rather than placing the burden on girls to escape child marriage. There was a lot of controversy over engaging men; a lot of pushback from some feminists who rightfully felt embittered by male oppression. But I think real change happens when we work as a collective, and, with regard to gender equality, no one is equal until we're all equal.

Five years later, we returned to the women who had taken part in the original research as we wanted to know if the positive impact was long-term or short-lived. We discovered that the interventions they had taken all those years before had inspired a healthier relationship with social media in the long term. Even though the toxic impact of social media among teens is worse now, when they connected with positive role models, we could show that their mental health improved, they felt better about themselves and they set higher personal and career goals. Participants called it 'transformative' and below are some of the key findings:

- Participants became more aware of how social media was affecting their mood and, as a result, were more careful users.
- The effect was long-lasting but was tied to the social-media platforms to which they had applied Disrupt Your Feed.
- Their career goals became more aspirational.
- They were using social media less overall.

- Participants reported that following new role-model suggestions from The Female Lead had expanded or reinforced their interests and aspirations.
- For the first group in 2018, feeling unable to measure up to the idealised images presented on social media was a major theme. For the second group, this was more muted.
- Participants were savvier about the manipulation of images and the fact that what was presented did not reflect reality.
- Participants in the second group would often 'take the lead in their own feed' and seek out inspirational models without further intervention.
- These results show that if we change what we are searching for and alter the algorithms, not only can the negative impacts be reversed, but social media can have a positive effect.

One of our participants in both of the Disrupt Your Feed (DYF) campaigns, Nida, told us about her experience of it afterwards.

I think it gave me a new perspective on social media. I ended up being able to regulate my use of social media much more effectively. Now I can see the content that I want to see and I feel like my relationship with social media is a lot more healthy. I follow people who I want to follow and people who inspire me. Having redone the study I can confidently say that DYF has really empowered my use of social media. I feel like I can really take ownership of my social-media use and I feel the content that I consume on social media is overwhelmingly positive. It's helped me in many ways. More ways than I can count. The DYF process has been extremely beneficial for me, it's helped me on my mental-health journey.

She said that having gone through the Disrupt Your Feed process, her social-media feed is now something that she consciously wants to look at and that she feels a lot more positive about and empowered by.

> Seeing people who almost have the perfect body on social media just felt very upsetting ... I just felt like I couldn't live up to that. By kind of disrupting my feed and being more aware of my social-media use and filtering out content that upset me, I was able to almost take control and reclaim my body image as my own.

Nida believes that social-media's algorithms can be an echo chamber and that social-media companies need to be more aware of this and the impact that the algorithms are having on younger people, especially as this demographic is so impressionable. She feels the way forward is to make people feel empowered by their use of social media and create positive change in that manner.

Disrupt Your Feed is one of the studies and campaigns I am most proud of. Through it, we showed how important role models are to girls and how these influences can change their mental health, self-worth and aspirations. When we see other people achieving what we didn't think was possible, we are able to raise the bar for what we can achieve.

This is where we will finish in Part III – with the macro and the women who have become influential figures in politics and corporations, and why diverse representation is so essential if we are ever going to see true equality.

Gina Martin, political activist and author

For the campaign, I applied all the principles of advertising. I continued to work full-time – I would get up at 5am to work on the campaign. I started with a social media post on Facebook to identify the group of guys. It went viral and I got a lot of abuse, including horrible messages from men saying they wanted to rape me. I was sure I was going to be kidnapped or hurt. We dehumanise such people and call them trolls, but they serve you coffee, work in your office and are the fathers of girls. I would look at their profiles and there would be a 35-year-old dad holding his daughter at a birthday party with his wife and friends.

During the campaign, I cried all the time – my brain couldn't deal with thousands of people shouting at me through my phone; I was having anxiety attacks and I went into therapy. I also kept on expecting the photos of my crotch to be released. To this day, those guys could still have the photos on their phone, which is humiliating, terrifying and repetitively traumatic. I got up every day and did the work but struggled in private. I couldn't stop: the fact that people thought it was okay to send abusive messages, was the very reason I had to continue.

For two years, I worked with a lawyer called Ryan Whelan and, in April 2019, we changed the Sexual Offences Act of 2003 to include upskirting, and introduced the Voyeurism Act.

What I find satisfying about activism is being part of something that's much bigger than myself. The purpose is like nothing I've ever felt before, but the struggle is like nothing I've ever felt before. But I can't do anything else. I can't go back to advertising and sell whisky: I just don't care, it's not important to me.

Everybody who does this work is putting themselves on the line, but some are risking far more than me: in many countries, you can't call yourself an activist because you'll get killed.

PART III

EMPOWERING WOMEN: THE BIG PICTURE

CHAPTER 13

THE BIG PICTURE

Women are not a minority, but when it comes to the top jobs in Government and large corporations, they still are. Significant progress has been made in the past hundred years, and the temptation can be to lean into this, which can often disguise what is still missing and needs to be done. If you are ever in doubt about whether equality has been achieved, just consider that only 8.2% of CEOs in the S&P 500 (the 500 largest publicly traded companies in the USA) are women.[1] The figures are even more alarming when it comes to the top governmental roles. Of the 193 members of the United Nations, only 13 have current leaders who are women, which is 6.7%.[2] When looking purely at statistics and data, nowhere is inequality clearer than when you look to the top.

I often hear men point out that more women go to university than men now and therefore equality has been achieved. I imagine they would like to cancel the campaign because they reckon that the job is done and equality is now in sight. This is when it pays to look a little closer at what this statistic really means. It is absolutely true that more women - 56.5% of universities' intake to be exact – go to university than men now.³ But what this shows is that, in general, women are driven, aspire to roles that require higher education and invest in a degree. The real tragedy is how this works out for them – all their effort, preparation and investment, but not much reward. Women are ambitious and want to step up, but the caregiving roles they accumulate as they grow older and other factors block them from progressing. So despite the female population having a higher rate of graduate education, the gender pay gap only widens as they get older. Despite their qualifications, the top jobs in corporations and Government are still decided by men and assigned to men.

I also often hear the comment that the pipeline of women is weak, which prevents more women from having the skills and experience to step up to the lead role. I am told that women are leaving the workplace around the age of 35, which causes an efficiency crisis and concern around leadership, progression and sustainability. But is it really a surprise that masses of women leave their jobs at this age when their work doesn't accommodate what else is often happening in their lives?

Women are half of the world's population, so until the decision-making roles and distribution of wealth reflect women's importance in society, change can only really be seen as superficial. Governments and large corporations make the decisions at a societal level, and men dominate these roles. Men do not, and should not, speak for women in all matters of power, control and influence. Money and power, which open up choice and freedom, drive our society, and if women do not have an equal share of these, then they do not have a voice. Without a clear voice, women become invisible, less understood and less valued. If women's wants and needs are not at the forefront, or even equally under-stood or considered, the danger is that their roles and rewards in society are taken for granted and given less respect or regard. Are women better at unpaid work or caring roles than men? Or is it that men would rather be paid for their work? Caring roles are critically important to our societal values and the lives of those around us. Yet they are underappreciated, undervalued and under-paid and, consequently, women are expected to fulfil them more than men.

As women, it's hard to understand why we do not have the same opportunities as men. Even though unequal rights were considered acceptable in the past, why is it still happening now? It seems extraordinary that women are still being told what they can and can't do with their bodies and that children are viewed as women's responsibility, when the reality is that men are involved in creating them and have custody rights.

We cannot wait for gradual changes to happen. The United Nations recently published an update on its goal of reaching gender equality by 2030.[4] Currently, 1 in 3 of all managers and supervisors are women, and reaching an equal number at our current rate of change will take another 140 years. Likewise, research into the S&P Global BMI (Board Market Index), holds women CEOs at 5.4% in 2022, up from 5% in 2021.[5] This research has calculated that at this expansion rate it would take around 111 years to reach an equal number of male and female CEOs.

I do not believe that women are less able than men. Rather, they are worn down, excluded and rejected many times by societal and organisational constructs. This is engrained in our language and daily lives – a language and behaviour that celebrates maleness. Professor Ian Robertson, states in his book, *How Confidence Works,* that:

> In general, people tend to rate men as more competent and confi-dent than women, with women being just as guilty of this bias as men. Those with a facial facade of competence end up as CEOs more often and are paid much more. It's important to note that they don't perform better than less competent-looking people. Their looks take precedence over actual outcomes, something that also happens with politicians. Unfortunately, this man-favouring bias in assessing confidence and competence happens across almost all cultures.

So, women themselves have become a part of the challenge to the rise of women as leaders and decision-makers. But, to acceler-ate our progress, we must have confidence that we belong in these rooms, making these decisions. Confidence begins with us knowing ourselves and what fulfils us and then focusing the time we can spare on building on these areas. If we all step forward and believe in ourselves and what we can do, the impact of that change will be far more significant than a few people trying to figure out how to alter something that has a deep inherent bias. Confidence should also be fuelled by the knowledge that our economic and decision-making powers are actually far greater than men's.

Through my work in data science, I discovered that women make, and still make, 70% of their household's buying decisions. Their influence can be even more significant as they often help with the purchasing decisions for other homes, such as relatives they care for. According to the *Harvard Business Review* women in America decide on the purchases of 94% of home furnishings,

92% of holidays, 91% of homes, 60% of cars and 51% of consumer electronics.[6] In the UK, household spending made up 61% of GDP in 2022, far more than the total of all the other categories, which included private investment, Government consumption and investment, and exports and imports of goods and services.[7] In the USA, private consumption sits at around 68%.[8] Women, therefore, are the largest group of consumers in the largest category of GDP. It makes both business and economic sense to build products and services for decision-makers. Yet, these organisations' leadership is currently full of men who are not the decision-makers in the vast majority of households and communities.

Women decide what is spent and what is bought, so they are theoretically a vital ingredient in any economy and in any decision about how life is lived or rewarded. And yet, we know that women often earn less than men. Our power-making authority is not recognised or reflected in our remuneration or social status. Women have been focused primarily on budgeting within agreed financial parameters. At the same time, men have been free to focus on one-off, long-term investment decisions or savings and largely free from the burden of everyday survival. In the first part of my career, every week I would enter the boardrooms of some of the world's largest retail and manufacturing companies, but there were no women in those rooms. Even though women make the majority of economic decisions in their households, they are not in positions of strategy, implementation or control in these vast organisations.

I don't expect leaders or organisations to respond to the argument that it is 'nice', 'fair' or 'the right thing to do' to have an equal number of women in the top jobs. It's not the type of language they necessarily respond to. Leaders have a clearly defined role: their job is to profitably create shareholder value and revenue by satisfying customer needs. Instead, I would tell them that female leaders make more sense than the current bias towards males because women make the purchasing decisions within households. As boardroom members, governmental leaders and heads of corporations, it makes absolute business sense that women hold 50% of these roles.

If women aren't part of the culture of how we organise companies or build brands, then we are not engaging women in the decisions that could make the difference between a business being really successful or not. This is fundamental. Women are likely to understand other women better than men. Women know what women want and understand how needs change over time, age by age. Women also increasingly want to buy from other women, and we see this happen more in business. Women are turning to female influencers who they are more likely to trust. An example of this is that women who are getting divorced or have been widowed want to have a female advisor. My mission is not to advocate for women because it's nice or fair. It's to advocate for women to be in these top jobs because it will make businesses and governments more successful and more knowledgeable about this distinctive and powerful 50% of their audience with the lion's share of buying power. This will, in turn, help organisations become better aligned with their audience and so create more revenue and more profit.

If businesses want to engage and sell to women, they need women to lead many of the decisions within the company as well. Today, companies use market research to understand women's spending habits, but market research can't always be relied on. From my data-science days and my work across the big, global supermarkets, I know that market research can only reflect answers to the questions you've thought to ask. The ground truth is never challenged. The huge leap forward in the retailing industry, which customer data revealed for the first time, is that 'You don't know what you don't know'. Data tells you the truth – honest opinions and behaviours – and some are hard to hear. But if, like Tesco, businesses want to double their market share within three years, it may be time to truly transform their leadership, especially in those powerhouse, decision-making roles.

If businesses responded to this, it would be a game-changer in terms of these institutions' strength and economic influence. Women are also incredibly profitable when in these roles. A report by S&P Global showed that firms with female CEOs and CFOs produced superior stock performance compared to the average.[9] In the two years after they were appointed, firms with female CEOs saw a 20% increase in stock-price momentum, and companies with a female CFO saw a 6% increase in profitability.

As women, we should draw confidence that from the point of view of our economic spending power, we are already driving the vast majority of decisions within our households and, therefore, for our countries. We are already decision-makers – we're just not being recognised or paid for it. If we take all the household choices made by the vast majority of women on a daily basis and scale them up, then women are equipped to do a similar thing on the macro level. We have generations of decision-makers who have been taught how to do this from a young age. Women are the missing ingredient in these positions of power and economic and political decision-making. We are valuable, and we are a necessity. It's not a nice thing that we have these roles. It's essential.

CHAPTER 14

ECONOMIC POWER

Even though I was CEO of my own company, our retail partners let it be known that they sometimes wanted my husband present, even though we had to take turns attending meetings so the other could look after our children. He was the Chief Scientific Officer (Data Scientist) and jokingly referred to as 'the genius'. They would ask if he would be at the meeting too, as if weighing up who made the most important contribution. I genuinely believe it took both of us to do what we did and that we were better together than alone. But I did wonder whether if he had been the CEO that question would have been considered or entertained. It wasn't until we were a billion-dollar company with 1,500 employees that I was seen as an expert and leader in my own right. I was very aware that, as a woman, I had to earn my place in these rooms.

For most of us, what happens in boardrooms is not something we spend much time thinking about. They are remote places that might conjure up images of wood-panelled rooms where, until recently, most people within them smoked cigars. Throughout my career in data, I have been in many of these rooms to talk to hundreds of boards about why they should hire my company.

These rooms came in all shapes and sizes, some with wall-to-wall glass, others enclosed and luxurious with paintings that were clearly investment pieces. Or, in the case of retailers, spartan and practical rather than inspiring. However, one thing that united them all was the absence of women. Invariably, these rooms would be stuffed full of men, and I would be the outsider.

When we interviewed Luiza Trajano, a remarkable woman who is the chair of a billion-dollar company, Magazine Luiza, she told us about her experiences as one of the few female retail company CEOs. She said:

> I have searched for female role models and I found some other female CEOs. We started to talk to each other and we started to meet. Now we have the group, Women of Brazil, which is focused on women's strength in education, culture and health. Women of Brazil has global goals, and one is the fight against violence. Violence is a problem in the whole world. It is everywhere, not only in Brazil.

She told us that her company has always been focused on diversity and they started to talk about quotas to encourage this.

> I am all for quotas as a transitory process to end inequality. We had been trying hard to get black people into senior positions. We had the idea of a trainee programme for black people and it was a success; we had 20,000 candidates. There was a lot of controversy on social media about the programme, for being 'reverse racism'. We were attacked on Twitter for 72 hours, but it created a shift and when you shift a paradigm, or a belief, you pay a price. Hiring women and black people is not a favour anymore. Companies that

don't change will not survive, because the market demands it. There is no innovation without it. You cannot have innovation if you don't sit at the table with different kinds of people.

Sallie Krawcheck, financial advisor for women, former CEO at Smith Barney, Citi Wealth Management and Merrill Lynch Wealth Management, former CFO at Citi
One reason why there are so few women in finance is because we tend to know few women in finance. It's not just that you can't see the door, you don't know where the door is – you don't even know there's a building. And once we know about it, it doesn't speak to us very much. We are as good at math as men – we know that. The challenge is that the industry doesn't present itself well. Young women perceive that the finance sector revolves around making money, scandal, gambling – and they go off to learn how to be, say, a paediatrician. I'd say finance is about helping families to live their lives, and pensioners to retire well. The industry has represented itself really badly as long as I've known it, but in fact there is a lot of purpose.

I firmly believe the businesses I was running were open to people from all sectors and backgrounds. However, the numbers on gender diversity in the US have not moved. If anything, they've gone backwards. I think that progress has been limited. I loved working on Wall Street. There was a straightforwardness to it, a sense of action, that I enjoyed for years. But Wall Street needs to be diverse and we need to provide a level playing field for everyone. We have a gender investing gap in this country – women do not invest like men do and you can't tell me that's not because of a gender gap in the industry.

In terms of women in business, we need to kiss the queen bee goodbye. We've had too many queen bees and I've been stung by them, as have my peers. I do get it. Historically, the research shows that if there was one woman at the table – and back then there probably was only one – you didn't want another woman to take your spot. My generation and the next one are rejecting that. The table can be bigger, we can get more chairs, and if there aren't enough chairs for us in corporate America, we can start our own businesses in a way we couldn't have done even five years ago.

Large corporations and their leaders influence so much of what happens in our world – their power and influence ranges far beyond one narrow area of business. They lobby governments for new laws, agree prices and distribution strategies and even decide what to acquire or what to shut down. They set the rate and balance between competitive pricing and the cost of production. This is likely to include offshore sourcing and complex supply chains that may reach into fragile and vulnerable communities. They also decide to what extent sustainability and environmental impacts are offset against profits and shareholder gains. All of these decisions affect the lives of millions of people – half of whom are women. When we don't have diversity in boardrooms, we have a single lens on what is both right and good for these companies and for society.

It is clear that when we get to the top of corporations, women do not have a leading role in them, and the data confirms this repeatedly. For example, in the UK, in 2022, only 8% of FTSE 100 businesses (the top 100 publicly traded companies) had a female CEO, and none were women of colour.[1] There are two reasons behind this: women are not being promoted to these positions in existing companies; or the companies women have founded do not receive the funding to expand and therefore remain as underinvested businesses.

Female-led start-up businesses are growing, but they are still trailing male-led entrepreneurial businesses. In 2022, 20% of all new businesses in the UK which were incorporated were all-female-led, an increase from 16% in the previous year.[2] This shows that women are increasingly setting up businesses but still at a rate lower than men. Research also shows that funding for all-women start-ups is less than for all-male start-ups, with the latter group receiving, on average, seven times more funding.[3] Therefore, the businesses that women set up are not being given the same chance of expanding as the ones created by men. Attempts to address this bias by financial services organisations include signing up to the Investing in Women Code, which was launched by the UK Government in 2019.

Baroness Helena Morrissey, who was CEO of Newton Investment Management from 2001 to 2016, felt so strongly about women's opportunities in business that she founded the 30% Club, a cross-business initiative aimed at achieving 30% female representation on UK corporate boards. She told us:

I believe strongly that you can create your own opportunities and one way of doing that is by asking for help when you don't have the answers. There are different ways of achieving and learning, and playing to your strengths, but asking for advice and making

sure you don't feel completely on your own is important. It's difficult to generalise, but women do tend to take the whole burden on
themselves. For men, how they ask for help might be discreet, but
they generally have a network they can call on if they're missing
something. I've never had a formal mentor, but I believe strongly
in the power of mentoring. I have lots of people whose opinions
I'm comfortable seeking, who will correct me if I'm wrong – again,
openness is important.

She explained that she subscribes to the idea of meritocracy –
but that the definition of merit can be very narrow.

Men develop networks and allegiances; women have a different
approach. The 30% Club was born out of frustration that so many
women are so capable and that isn't recognised. The homogeneity
of boards and management teams was definitely a contributory
factor to the financial crisis. People were too insular, they weren't
questioning each other, they had been to the same schools, they
were friends. This isn't just about women. Men are involved in the
30% Club too; men on boards who want to see a different boardroom dynamic. We want to further a cultural shift in businesses
and organisations.

**Christine Lagarde, President of the European Central
Bank and former Managing Director of the International
Monetary Fund from 2011 to 2019**
Unfortunately, I am often the only woman in the room. There are
a few more women than there were 10 or 15 years ago but

finance is still a very male-dominated environment. We are dealing with banks, financial experts, economists, finance ministers and governors of central banks, and in most instances these people are men. I do not think that I am treated differently but I probably had a harder time establishing credibility and being respected, whereas for men these are taken for granted instantly. The probation period for women is probably a little longer and the probation tests are probably a little harder.

We all like to be liked and being criticised is hard, but you just accept it. You fix it when it is legitimate, you ignore it when it is completely gratuitous, or full of hatred – you move on. Occasionally, I compare with other women and very often we have faced and experienced the same issues. We had to prove ourselves and overcome the almost inherent lack of confidence that I do not think men experience as much as we do . . .

If there is a collective will to include women – and that is often the case – then there has to be a good analysis of what the situation is, what the numbers are, what the education level is, what the opportunities can be, and what the obstacles may be along the way. Once that map has been drawn, then every effort should be made to remove the obstacles, improve opportunities, support education and set targets. Now, whether you call these targets quotas or participation rates in the labour market does not really matter. But to have objectives, and ways to measure against those objectives, I think is necessary. I used to be against quotas when I was much younger, thinking, 'Why should we not just succeed and participate on our own merits?' Unfortunately, there is such a long way to go that targets, quotas and accountability are needed in order to bridge that gap.

One of the solutions for how to get women into the board-rooms of corporations is gender quotas. This is when a company or even a government determines that there should be a minimum number of women in prominent positions within a company. A recent example of this is the French Government making it mandatory for corporations to have a certain number of women on their boards. On paper, this sounds like a great initiative and the direction all corporations should be taking. However, the interpretation around what this means and the impact are more nuanced than anticipated.

The argument for quotas is controversial. On one hand, it is an opportunity for innovation of thought and approach. On the other, many women want to feel that they've arrived at the top and are in a position of power through talent and hard work, not via a quota system. However, we do know that if we leave appointments and promotions to the current processes, there won't be any improvement or change. Women need a helping hand to the top even when they have all the skill and talent required because it just doesn't happen naturally.

But when we drill down into the roles these women are given to fulfil quotas, they don't often come with much power. Not all boardroom positions are equal, or come with the same level of influence or even decision-making rights. Often these quotas are filled by giving women non-executive director roles, which means they are not involved in the company's day-to-day running. In 2022 in the UK, 91% of women on FTSE 100 boards were in non-executive director roles.[4] It is yet another example of women trying to step up but not being treated equally and instead being so quietly, and often charmingly, reduced. Even when women are given decision-making roles, they will typically be in Human

Resources or Marketing rather than being appointed the CEO, CFO or Commercial Director.

When women get to the executive positions, known as the 'C-Suite', they are also often paid differently to men. C-Suite roles obviously come with a salary and other benefits, but there is the opportunity to have shares in the company as well. Shares are crucial because ownership of them is another controlling force in the direction a business takes. Unfortunately, when it comes to securing shares in companies, the gender gap is huge. At The Female Lead, we did our own research into this, and the results were startling. Of the top executives at S&P 500 companies, women only have around 1% of the value of shares held amongst its leaders.[5] Therefore, despite women being brought into executive roles, they do not have anywhere near the same shareholding power as the men around them.

This gender gap in shareholding is seen at all levels of wealth. If we travel upwards to the world's richest people, the billionaires, only 12% of them are women.[6] Of that 12%, nearly 70% of those women inherited their wealth rather than being classed as self-made, meaning they founded or cofounded a business or created their wealth in another way.

Another area where women do not have equal representation is in media or entertainment companies. Research shows that in the early and managerial levels of these companies, women have an equal number of roles in the USA.[7] However, once we reach the C-Suite level, this number falls to 27%. In social-media companies, female representation among the boards of directors in 2022 was 40% at Meta, 33% at Pinterest, 33% at Snapchat, 27% at Twitter, 18% at YouTube and 12.5% at We-Chat.[8] At the time of writing, none of the CEOs of these companies were women.

Equal representation in media, entertainment and social-media companies is essential because these huge corporations decide what young girls and women see on a daily basis. If female representation in the media is diverse, girls grow up with a wide range of influences. If it is narrow, and they are only fed cookie-cutter stereotypes of women, it limits their view of their own opportunities or freedom to express themselves. A similar thing happens as women age. Research has shown that fewer than 1 in 4 characters on top-grossing domestic films and the most popular television shows in the USA, between 2010 and 2020, were 50 years old or over.[9] Of those 1 in 4 characters over the age of 50, women made up only 20% of film characters and 25% of broadcasted television programmes. As women age, they slip from our view on screens, and this reinforces the notion that women only have media value when they are young.

Whichever way you look at it, women don't have an equal share of money, influence or decision-making power at all levels within companies. Although quotas open up these boardrooms to women, there is a real danger that all of this is done to comply with those quotas, and that the roles women are appointed to, although senior, are most definitely not the key power-holder or decision-making ones except in rare instances. Quotas are also liable to come and go as they rely on targets, priorities and policy changes, both in business and government. Quotas are a legitimate method of opening up these rooms to women, but they are not the most compelling route. A far more convincing one is showing leaders that they should appoint women to positions of influence because it improves their businesses performance.

If we look at retail spend, at least 70% of the household purchase decisions are made by women. Yet the person in the boardroom, including the powerhouse decision-maker who is usually the Commercial Director, is invariably a man. The Commercial Director will decide which products are the most important, what they stock, how much they stock and what price they are sold for. The Commercial Director will decide what women want to buy. Yes, there will be testing and market research, but in truth most of these focus groups are simply to adjust a product or offer. If we also look at social-media companies, they have boards that are heavily weighted towards men but, in the UK, 51.6% of all social-media users are women.[10] Globally, women spend, on average, 62.59 minutes each day on social-media apps, while men only spend 49.53 minutes.[11] Again, decisions on what women see and the responsibilities these companies have towards their users are largely being made by men.

Beyond the commercial benefit to companies and the economy, if women are in these guiding roles, they can implement policies that help other women rise through all the ranks of a business. The innate constructs of a company that place a glass ceiling above women and trap men can be overhauled. They can be changed into a model that is more suitable for our modern society, where it is likely that in most households both people either work or want to work.

*   *   *

If corporations have the potential to influence governments, then it is the people within governments who decide which corporations they listen to. Nowhere is societal change so influential as in the role of Government, and also nowhere is a lack of women in the top jobs clearer.

Limor Fried, electrical engineer and founder of Adafruit

It's a challenge to start a company. I went in blindly, not thinking how hard it would be, but I've done it. We give everybody the opportunity to grow, half the directors are women, and we're always hiring people and giving them a chance. What I like about running a company is that I get to make those decisions. If I had a venture company or investors backing me, they'd say, 'This is too risky.' Running a company is scary but if it's your own company, you can run it how you want to, and all the things you hate about companies, you can choose not to do.

Adafruit is awesome. I enjoy going into the factory every day, working with amazing people, seeing them flourish. Everyone in the company gets along. At the end of meetings, tech companies normally have a bug report. We have a hug report, where people give a shoutout to someone who's helped them – covered their hours, helped them with a project. It's really positive. Instead of creating a culture of backstabbing, if we all raise each other up, it's better for everyone. We invite people to come and see these weekly meetings and they go away saying, 'I'm going to do that in my company' – we're trying to create a viral model of not being crappy to each other.

I'm a leader, but I'm not the boss – the customers and the people I work with dictate what I do every day. I've offloaded so much of my task to the people I work with but they still have to tell me what they need, and for the customers, it's my job to give them a good experience. My philosophy is that the DNA of the company flows from the leadership – the owner sets the culture. It's really important to set an example, because how the leader acts is how everyone is going to act.

CHAPTER 15

DECISION-MAKING POWER

When we had the opportunity to interview Christine Lagarde, who is currently the President of the European Central Bank and was Managing Director of the International Monetary Fund from 2011 to 2019, she had many wise thoughts to share, but the following really resonated with me:

> I have often observed in many instances that when a society, a corporate organisation or a community is in crisis, very often women are called upon to help, support, fix and rebuild. In times of crisis, very often I see women taking the lead, taking the helm. A good friend of mine who used to be Governor of a central bank in Africa used to say, 'Men go to war and women come afterwards to fix it.' Very often, in times of crisis, we call the women!

For meaningful change to happen with regard to women's equality, we have to look to the top of the decision-making roles to facilitate this. Nowhere does this happen more rapidly and widely than if it becomes law. Up until 1975, when the Equal Pay Act came into force, it was still legal to pay women less than men for the same work. This statute hasn't eradicated the gender pay gap, but it has stopped employers from blatantly paying women less money for equal work. Laws don't always prevent illegal acts, but they do shift the foundations of what is seen as acceptable in society. The Equal Pay Act has made it illegal for women to be paid less than men for the same work, and on this basis has brought to the forefront the gender pay gap. If we take a moment to think about what laws would help women step into the room and stay there, the list is inspiring. What would the world look like if men got longer, fully paid paternity leave? Or quality childcare was provided and subsidised by the Government that matched people's working hours? Or children had a programme of meeting inspiring role models introduced into their curriculum?

Women are not all the same and have different needs depending on their circumstances, personalities and ambitions. All these contrasting needs will not be considered until we have a diverse group of women representing us in the top government roles. At the moment, it is very easy for a government to point to one specific policy change and pronounce that they've helped 'women', when instead, they have helped a small group of women. The difficulty with women entering these top decision-making roles is that it is a closed loop. Women aren't present in these rooms because their needs aren't considered, and until their needs are considered, they will have a more difficult time entering the rooms.

Joyce Banda, President of Malawi from 7 April 2012 to 31 May 2014

I didn't plan to end up in politics. I believe that leadership is a love affair. You must fall in love with the people and the people must fall in love with you. I fell in love with the rural people and the underprivileged people of this country at a very young age. There's a lot of power in the people there, and, when they love you, they stand for you through thick and thin.

Those of us who are my age must reach out and help the younger ones. We have had so many challenges in our lives; we must provide support to the younger ones so that they don't go the hard way, like we did. If you listen to Julia Gillard, the misogyny in Australia is very similar to the to the misogyny in Africa. Our challenges have been the same. I always say to African women that they must not get discouraged, because in the whole world women are facing the same challenges. What we need to do is stand up and say, 'Somebody has to do it.' We cannot chicken out, we cannot say we will not do it and leave our brothers to proceed. I have always said the reason why Africa has done so well in getting women into positions of leadership, of presidency, is because we have agreed that we will participate in leadership, but we will do it our way: our understanding of feminism must be African. Your understanding of feminism is your own, and we must respect one another.

My task now is to encourage all African women who make it to support younger girls. Women make the best leaders because they face challenges, they take risks, and they're fearless, they're sincere and they're compassionate.

In the UK, we have recently had two female prime ministers within seven years. This is an achievement in itself, but I also want to look at the broader picture, which tells a very different story. Of the 193 countries the United Nations recognises, only 13 currently have a female head of government. Of these 13 countries, only 4 have previously had women leaders.[1] This means that, in 2023, only 6.7% of countries have female leaders and 93.3% have male leaders. When we look at the all-time number, less than a third of countries have ever had a female leader. This means that a quarter of the way through the 21st century, in over two-thirds of the countries where girls are taught about their history, they cannot learn about a single female leader of their country in modern times. Some of the most populous countries of the world are included in this list: China, the United States of America, Nigeria, Russia, Mexico, Japan, France and Spain, to name a few. That is a lot of girls growing up without role models who hold the top position of decision-making power.

The argument for having 50% female politicians in our governments, cabinets and top leadership roles is that they represent 50% of the population. The definition of democracy is that elected *representatives* hold positions of power. If women have fewer of these positions than men, how can women's needs be truly represented or even considered? If a government cannot represent its people, then surely, using all logical arguments, it must be failing.

To begin answering what is stopping women from stepping into these roles, we need to shift down two levels to the women who are active politicians and our potential future leaders. In the UK in 2023, women made up 35% of all MPs, an increase from 17.9% in 2001 and 3.5% in 1983.[2] So we are heading in the right direction when it comes to female representation in Parliament, but it is still not equal. But when it comes to the top jobs of being in the prime minister's cabinet, our current representation drops to 25%.[3] According to the United Nations, on a global basis, women hold 22.8% of cabinet positions leading policy decisions. The type of roles they hold in these positions is also telling.[4] The same research shows the five most commonly held policy-deciding roles women hold are women and gender equality, family and children's affairs, social inclusion and development, social protection and social security, and indigenous and minority affairs.

UK politics is generally dominated by men who are in closed networks, which can often be traced back to their schools and universities. Large parts of our government, and many others, have a 'boys club' culture. Governments often say that they want to elevate women but their reason for being unable to do this is that there aren't the numbers in the wings. One of the reasons there are fewer female than male politicians is that while these potentially toxic networks exist, they put women off from pursuing a career in politics. It becomes a cycle of women not wanting to be there because it is a male-dominated environment, with men falling back on the lack of candidates as an excuse.

Another issue that female politicians are contending with more than ever is the constant misogyny and abuse they face through social media or other online communications, and minority ethnic women particularly face these attacks. Rape and death threats are common. These attacks are not harmless as they affect mental health, and there is always the additional fear for personal safety and that of their family. This fear is also not unfounded. In the past seven years, two MPs in the UK, Jo Cox and Sir David Amess, were murdered when meeting with their constituents.

Other factors preventing women from entering or remaining in politics are childcare and maternity leave. In the UK, there is an ongoing battle for female MPs to have paid maternity leave, and it is only recently that women could hire a locum to cover their duties to constituents. Since 1979, the average age for a newly elected male MP is 41.2, but for women it is 44.4.[5] This age gap clearly shows that women have to wait longer to enter Parliament, which is likely because they have childcare responsibilities they feel they have to deal with first. Ultimately, this means that women may feel forced to choose between having children and being a politician.

There have been a few raised eyebrows when women have taken newborns into Parliament, but also a lot of support for it from both male and female MPs. Despite this general support, in 2022, a committee report stated that MPs should not be allowed to bring babies into the House of Commons. This raises the question of what is so intolerable about a woman bringing a baby to their work environments. During a debate, MPs were quoted as saying that MP Stella Creasy's baby was 'as good as gold' when she took him into the House of Commons. If a baby isn't disrupting proceedings, what is the problem about a woman bringing them into the room? Is it an offensive sight? Or is it one that reminds people that there is a life outside work? If the baby starts disturbing proceedings, that's a different matter, and it is likely that many mothers would exit the room until the child was quieter. If the argument is that having a child there doesn't reflect the gravitas of proceedings, then why is no one raising an eyebrow at men making deals worth millions or even billions of dollars when driving around in golf buggies? Yet again, the standards are unequal, and women are often on the back foot just because of having children.

Besides facilitating women being present in the room, having babies around is a clear representation of what many women are going through – juggling work with childcare and trying to treat both as equally important. Perhaps the real reason this is viewed as inappropriate is because it is a visual reminder of what so many women are contending with. It is a reminder of women's competing roles, and it is easier for people to turn away rather than tackle it.

*   *   *

When women have an equal share in economic and decision-making power, the world will be changed. More diversity of input leads to more diversity of thought. What would that world look like, and, of equal importance, when will we know we have reached true gender equality?

Julia Gillard, 27th Prime Minister of Australia

When I became Deputy Prime Minister and then Prime Minister, there was no missing the fact that I was the first woman in those jobs. On my first day as Prime Minister, the media ran reports about what I was wearing rather than what I said. Female politicians are always asked about family structures – and there's no right answer. If you have kids, people ask who's looking after them and whether you can do a big job. If you don't have kids, and I don't, people wonder whether you really understand family life. But the essence of politics is that you've got so much to do. There's not a moment to waste. You want to make the maximum amount of change you can in the time you are there. So I didn't dwell on it; I got on with the job.

When I gave what's come to be known as 'the misogyny speech', I had no idea it would resonate outside the parliamentary chamber, let alone that we'd still be talking about it all these years later. I think the speech has come to represent for many women a sort of battle anthem. It keeps finding a new audience because, unfortunately, women still have to navigate a very sexist world.

The rhythms of politics have been built around men's rather than women's lives. And then there are all the sexist stereotypes that swirl in our heads about women leaders. Many of the women Ngozi Okonjo-Iweala and I talked to for our book were conscious of being on a tightrope. If they came across as too tough, people would think, 'Oh, she doesn't seem very likeable'. But if they came across as too kind and empathetic, people would think, 'She seems nice, but she clearly lacks the backbone for the job.' I do think this leads to a set of self-limiting behaviours; women leaders live with that voice in their heads telling them to be careful about their behaviour.

CHAPTER 16

WHAT THIS WORLD COULD LOOK LIKE

We live in a world that is developing at an accelerating pace. We all find ourselves charging forwards into the unknown, whether we are ready for it or not. The technological, scientific and political developments we face require a society that matches or even outstrips their progress so we can retain control and pre-empt the challenges of tomorrow. This is where we fall down. We cannot keep up with these changes if half of our population is not equally represented in the decisions being made. The advancement of gender equality has moved further and faster in the past hundred years than at any other time in our recorded history. However, this equality still repeatedly falls short of where we need to be. As I write this in 2023, the gender gap in almost every area of life is still pronounced. In many spheres, it has plateaued, and in some, such as women's access to abortion, it is going backwards. This mustn't be as good as it gets for women or, even worse, we end up sliding backwards into roles of subservience and submission. Women know that they deserve to be in the room, being heard, making decisions and leading the way forward. Women do not need *fixing*, because they are not the problem.

We cannot fall back on the current trajectory rate for equality because we do not know what world we will live in by the time we reach it. We do not have a spare hundred years to give away. Instead, this gap needs to be closed swiftly by starting with the self, focusing on what fulfils us, projecting this into our communities and finally stepping into the macro roles of decision-making and economic power. When women have a more equal platform, they can make a fundamental and game-changing contribution to the economy. This future of equal power and wealth is one worth striving and fighting for. It is one of diversity of thought, tolerance of others and sustainability. In essence, it is enduring.

When we consider what this world would look like if that were the case, it would not be based on a hunch, anecdotal evidence or assumption. Instead, it would be grounded in data. Also, when we look to this future, it will not be built on women's gains equating to men's losses. There is room at the table for everyone, and we can always add more seats if necessary.

The most significant change in women's roles in the past century is an increase in their paid employment. On top of this, the lion's share of caring roles still fall to women. Making the two work smoothly together is usually impossible because we operate in work environments which have been designed by men, and are antiquated and no longer fit for purpose. They were created at a time when men worked predominantly, while women stayed at home. It was also a time when a village helped raise a child, and there were often older siblings or cousins around to help care for younger children. Nowadays, most households require and often want two incomes, and our work hours and holiday provision do not match schooling hours. There is very little free or affordable afterschool, preschool or holiday care for our children. Because of this, women either have to pay a premium for their children to be cared for, cut down their working hours (and increase their lifelong money gap) or rely on the help of relatives and friends if it is available.

If more women were in decision-making roles in government, it is likely they would tackle the childcare crisis. Our data shows that childcare provision is what women aged 35–44 are focused on in the Work pillar of satisfaction. Research also shows a direct causal relationship between the number of women on municipal councils in Norway and childcare provision.[1] This issue hasn't yet been fully addressed in most countries because it has mainly been men making the decisions on it or ignoring it completely. If more women were in the room contributing to the ethos of how businesses were run or how the government organises childcare provision, they would use their own experiences of juggling work and childcare commitments, or the experiences of women around them, to inform their decisions. This also applies to unpaid care that women provide to elderly relatives, which will only increase as our population ages.

If childcare and caring provisions don't reduce or prevent our ability to work, it will mean that women won't have to choose between their relationships and work. Research shows that 45% of women who care for others would want to take on more work hours, which would boost the earnings of female carers by £28.4 billion each year.[2] This would mean more taxable income and increased money in households and the economy. The financial responsibility for a family unit would also be more evenly split between couples, and women's jobs and careers would then be seen as equally important to men's. It might then be decided that it makes more financial sense for the men in mixed-sex relationships to stay at home and take extended paternity leave. These changes will also give men more freedom of choice, and they will no longer be trapped by the working environments that limit women's ability to reach their full potential.

Research also shows that women give more to charity than men, with 72% of women in the UK reporting having donated money in 2021/22, compared to 61% of men.[3] This indicates that if the gender pay gap and money gap were closed, more money would be donated to charities as women would have more disposable funds. On an extreme scale of this, MacKenzie Scott, the former wife of Jeff Bezos, the third wealthiest person in the world, has given more money away in the two years since her divorce than her ex-husband has done in his entire lifetime. Similar to charitable giving, there is voluntary work to consider. If our workplaces better accommodate the needs of its employees, there would also be the opportunity for men and women to provide more voluntary work in areas that are important to them.

Our own research shows the importance of the environment to women. In the Society pillar of fulfilment, it is a topic that women aged 35–54 particularly care about, perhaps because they are concerned about what future generations will face. It is therefore likely that women in positions of power would set environmentalism as part of their agenda. When it comes to the environment, we are currently passing the point of no return. We cannot afford to wait a hundred years until governments and corporations have an equal number of women in decision-making roles. Every year is crucial and will impact future generations and the challenges they face. If the worst that scientists have warned us about does happen, many girls and women of tomorrow could be in a situation where they won't be able to consider what fulfils them as they will have a daily struggle to find clean water and food. When it comes to the urgency for immediate change, what happens to the world we live in and what enables our survival are some of the most pressing matters. Governments and businesses decide our trajectory for this. Without diversity of thought, we will continue to approach our environment as something that will provide infinite resources rather than something we must care for and replenish. Research shows that women are better leaders in a crisis.[4] I am certain that they will also be better at preventing a crisis too.

In a global arena, if more CEOs were women, it would provide a diversity of thought while also being beneficial for businesses and the economy. As we have discussed previously, companies run by female CEOs see an increase in stock-price momentum and firms with a female CFO show an increase in profitability. Alongside their financial acumen, female CEOs lead differently from their male counterparts. Research shows that women CEOs' communication styles are much more positive than men's, with an emphasis placed on diversity, empathy and adaptability.[5] Our own research shows that women consider integrity and the ability to show vulnerability as qualities of a good leader.

In a recent poll on LinkedIn, we asked our audience, 'What is the most important quality of a leader?' We received 80,287 votes, and the responses were as follows:

- Integrity: 52%
- Empathy: 32%
- Vision: 11%
- Decisiveness: 5%

In another poll we held on LinkedIn, we asked, 'How important is it for leaders and managers to show vulnerability?' We received 30,215 votes, with the following replies:

- Essential: 63%
- Somewhat important: 32%
- Not important: 5%

We have reached a time when some businesses have more wealth and power than governments and countries. If regulations and boundaries struggle to control them, then we must look to their leaders for either their agreement to abide by the rules or to create their own self-regulation. If the leadership styles of female CEOs are different from men's and emphasis is placed on empathy, positivity and diversity, then these are the characteristics of the people who we should want to trust with the immeasurable power that now often comes with being one of the world's largest conglomerates.

When it comes to these giant organisations, many of them are social-media or media companies with the power to influence billions of people's lives, views and opinions. My husband and I always used the phrase, 'You are what you eat' about supermarket data. I now believe it can also apply to our relationship with social media. The content we consume every day shapes who we are and, with children, the people they will become. If our social-media and television channels are filled with impossible beauty standards, we will raise a generation of insecure, image-obsessed women (and also men), who often feel that they have fallen short somehow. At The Female Lead, we have already shown through our research the transformative power of girls and women taking the lead in their own life by regulating the content they consume and follow. Think of the changes that would also arise if the algorithms showed a wider variety of content, or if more was done to limit the potentially harmful information that is so regularly accessible to children. Who would that generation grow up to be? What decisions would they then make as leaders?

The same applies to media companies, which still have a huge impact on our influences. The media's fixation on what they deem 'photogenic' leaders pushes aside all women who don't meet this criterion. We have all seen the media reporting on female leaders' clothes rather than their policies. This fuels both the public's interest in women's appearances and mutes the voices of our women leaders. The Female Leads we have interviewed rise by lifting others. If women were the head of these media companies or in decision-making roles, they would likely place the message of female leaders above the minutiae and platform a more diverse selection of women for readers and viewers to access.

We also have to consider the role Artificial Intelligence (AI) will play in our future and the content we consume. AI is informed by what is already available – the data which it relies on to create an optimum targeting model of what good looks like. If there is a lack of female role models at the source, then there will be a lack of female role models featured in the future. It will replicate the bias wherever we have no prominent women leaders, CEOs, entrepreneurs or government leaders. All of these tools will learn from what is currently available, which is what students and the general population already rely on so heavily.

The same thing happened before to women in another arena. For centuries, women were excluded from medical research, so what we have is a set of research based on male anatomy. Similarly, we are now on the brink of having vast swathes of our future content founded on the current bias towards male leaders. We are repeating the same pattern and cycle to the detriment of women.

Now is the time to change this and bring to the forefront the multitude of women doing extraordinary things. Women tend to be more modest than men and won't shout about what they are doing. They just get on and do it. This is why it is so important that The Female Lead is building the most extensive panel on women's data, because data on women is the ground truth, and now is the time to collect it and ensure that the algorithms don't blindly take us where we have already been.

*   *   *

The Female Lead wants to help empower women of all ages, but we are particularly interested in the influences that girls and young women are growing up with. This is because we know that they are our potential future leaders and that these formative years greatly impact women's overall self-belief. I am confident that if women were really in positions of wealth and power, there would be more balanced wisdom regarding how we operate as a country and as a group of businesses. If the next generation believes that they can and should be leaders, this is much more likely to happen. Therefore, education is key.

I hope that in the future, our schools will be permitted to measure their success on more than just grades and that they also help prepare students for jobs of the future with up-to-date careers advice, as well as measure students' happiness and fulfilment. It is unheard of for a business to measure its performance on only one

Key Performance Indicator, so why do we place so much emphasis on exam results and only measure grades and not subjects? Surely all subjects are not equal to our future success. If children enjoy their time at school, this is much more likely to encourage them to be lifelong learners who can more easily adapt to the multiple career changes that so many of us now have. The topics and life skills they learn about can also help them prepare for a future of uncertainty. When we look at women's relationship with money, it would be particularly helpful if both girls and boys were taught about handling finances from a young age.

It would also be vastly beneficial if a diverse range of modern female role models were woven into the curriculum. We seem to be fixated on past role models such as Florence Nightingale, Ada Lovelace and Amelia Earhart. The contribution these women made to their fields was enormous, but there are women here, right now, who are also doing the same. Do we have to wait another 80 years for their achievements to be taught to children? The longer we wait to learn about them in schools, the more distant they become in time and circumstance. This means that girls and boys do not see these historical figures as their contemporaries and do not see themselves as the next part of the equation. Young girls have to be able to imagine themselves belonging and wanting to be in these places of influence. Young boys need the opportunity to see women doing as many inspiring things as men. Role models need to be relatable – not old and dead.

What we believe about ourselves is often the most significant limiting factor to who we are and what we want to become. If children don't hear the right language or see the right role models, these opportunities are taken away. The results could be transformative if we had contemporary female role models being taught about in schools and even potentially visiting them. If children accumulate a different set of values and beliefs about male and female roles, and how they can cross over and blend, our future leaders will build on this foundation and the trajectory for equality will accelerate.

Work on these things should begin now, as the need for change is urgent if we are to prevent ourselves from sliding backwards. We should also not be distracted by unique wins in distinct areas that have the potential to derail us from true equality across all areas of life. If the gender pay gap is closed, let's refocus on the money gap. If there are an equal number of female CEOs to male ones, let's look at where we are with gender-based violence. One win is a step forward but not the final destination. For me, I will always look to the data in all areas to know if we have achieved true equality.

I was once told that we will only attain true equality when there are as many incompetent women in boardrooms as there are incompetent men. This might make you smile, but there is also a truth to it. When we look around the rooms where the decisions are being made, and there are not just a small number of women present who represent the best of the best, or are the most well-connected, or feel that they have to emulate what are seen as masculine characteristics, we will have made an immense stride forwards. The representatives in these rooms will either only stand for a narrow band of people or ensure that everyone is present.

There is also another way that will prove to me that we have reached true equality and its future is secure. It will be when I walk into a school and ask the children who their role models are. If half the boys raise their hands and name a female role model who they aspire to be, that will be a quantum step forward into a new era, promising long-lasting change.

BE EMPOWERED

One of my strengths is seeing the greatness in others, and I firmly believe that everyone has at least one superpower that will benefit the world and potentially change it. There's not much room for modesty when it comes to these gifts, and they should be acknowledged, nurtured and explored. If we think of ourselves as the source of our talents, like a light beam, the further we push our talents into the world, the wider their reach. If more of us worked to our strengths, the world would be a more productive and fulfilling place. We would be more confident in ourselves and our contribution, and this would enable us to step into the room and make our voices heard.

It is very easy to say what is wrong with gender equality. Although it needs to be highlighted continuously so that it is less easily dismissed, there also has to be a path to overcome it. That path starts with ourselves, focusing on our strengths, and with uniting or creating other communities. We can then explore what fulfils us and concentrate on improving the areas that are most important to us. The final destination will be entering the decision-making rooms, leaving the door open for other women to follow until we fill half of the seats and represent half the population.

There was a saying among retailers, known as 'good, better, best', which meant there should be different ranges to cover all customers' needs. They recognised that all of these different levels were required and relevant as we each have different resources and tastes. This is a saying I have continued to use throughout both of my careers. We can also apply it when we want to make a change, as we each have different commitments and ambitions.

How to be In the Room

Empowerment on the Individual Level

- Become inspired: explore the qualities you admire and the beliefs you buy into.
- Know yourself: find out about your strengths and concentrate on developing these.
- Celebrate strengths: celebrate your and others' strengths, and find a community to align with.

Empowerment through Fulfilment

- Find out what fulfils you and what you are passionate about.
- Explore where you are lacking fulfilment in the areas that are important to you.
- Concentrate on increasing these areas.

Empowerment on the Macro Level

- Become a leader in the area you are passionate about and that fulfils you.
- Help others to rise as you do.
- Step into the decision-making roles that shape our businesses and society.

The 'good, better, best' theory can also apply to how far we can take these three steps. If every girl or woman who reads this book decided to spend some time learning about what they admire, their innate talents and finding a community – even a community of two – we would have a new cohort with strengthened confidence and self-belief, whose voices were united with others.

If members of that group decided to explore what fulfilled them and what they were passionate about, there would be a contingent of women and girls who had found their purpose in life and would begin pushing that into their communities and bringing others with them.

We would then have a vast swathe of women with the self-belief and direction to step into rooms on the macro level. They would be able to move into decision-making roles that represent the needs of half the population and shape our society and the direction we are moving in. The door would be open for other women to follow and true equality would finally be within our reach.

ACKNOWLEDGEMENTS

I have been able to create this new book because of you, our brilliant Female Lead audience. You engage with us, whatever our subject, whatever the questions we ask of you. Thank you for your passion, your trust and most of all your belief. I remain committed to finding a better path for women so that we can all feel more fulfilled in life and work.

I want to thank specifically all the amazing people I've worked with over the years. It's been a privilege and a lot of hard work, but has also involved much fun and comradeship. Hearing the stories of amazing women has created a wealth of ideas and recommendations that I've learned and benefited from personally. I hope others will benefit too as I share the best of that advice and some of my own pains and triumphs.

I want to take this moment to pay tribute to the wonderful influencers who have supported us and taken up our pledges and campaigns – thank you. I want to acknowledge our academic partners who have collaborated with us across a number of critical and ground-breaking research projects. In particular, I want to highlight the work of Dr Terri Apter, who identified the value and significance of what we were exploring some five years ago at Cambridge University, and who has already helped us to understand and develop simple but powerful interventions to improve mental health among teens. Dr Eamon Fulcher has been an invaluable advisor to us on neuroscience, cognitive diversity and our headline focus on the science of fulfilment.

My old colleagues from dunnhumby and more recently Starcount are simply the best when it comes to predicting what people want and need. I am proud and excited to continue that pioneering work. This book signals another important landmark, new data and research we've been privileged enough to collect on what women want. This insight is the key to real transformation that can and will elevate women to the status and influence they deserve across all parts of society. We now have the evidence; we just need the bold pioneers alongside.

I want to thank my wonderful publisher Rose Sandy and agent Rachel Mills who were excited from the start about what we were revealing and activating at The Female Lead. Much has been said about the challenges and difficulties that women face, but what they both recognised was our unique ability to create new perspectives and tools around why women matter and to quantify the true value they bring to business and society. Our mission at The Female Lead is to present new data and evidence to leadership so that change becomes a 'must have', not just a polite nod to women.

I want to pay tribute to my incredibly hardworking and talented team: Rowena Humby (not only my amazing team lead but also a trustee of our educational foundation); Lauren Lind (Studio and Content); Holly Francis (Data and Science); Veryan Dexter (Research and Learning); Paddy Spiers (Filming and Editing); Izzy De Almeida (Filming and Editing); and last but never least,

Laura Whiteside (all-round superstar). Together we are small but mighty.

Finally, I want to thank my life and work partner, Clive Humby, who is always there for me, believing in what I do but adding his skills and expertise whenever the challenge is great. He still has the magic touch when it comes to data and storytelling!

NOTES

CHAPTER 1: THE POWER OF TWO: DATA AND STORIES

1. 'Making better decisions in groups', *R Soc Open Sci.* 2017 Aug; 4(8): 170193.
2. 'Women Count 2022: the role, value and number of female executives in the FTSE 350', The Pipeline.
3. *British Labour Statistics Historical Abstract 1886-1968*, Table 109, escoe. ac.uk.
4. 'Employment rate in the United Kingdom from 1st quarter 1971 to 2nd quarter 2023, by gender', statista.com
5. 'Women CEOs run more than 10% of Fortune 500 companies for the first time in history', fortune.com.

CHAPTER 8: RELATIONSHIPS

1. 'What women want: tackling gender equalities in unpaid care and the workplace', progressive-policy.net.
2. 'Men and women have differing views on the domestic and career impacts of having a child', harris.uchicago.edu.
3. 'Gender division of housework during the COVID-19 pandemic: temporary shocks or durable change?', demographic-research.org.
4. 'Net childcare costs', data.oecd.org.
5. 'Weekly childcare costing some parents more than half of their take-home pay, new analysis shows', bitc.org.uk.

6. 'Women in the labour market: boosting mothers' employment and earnings through accessible childcare', progressive-policy.net.
7. 'Living longer: caring in later working life: examining the interplay between caring and working in later life in the UK', ons.gov.uk.

CHAPTER 9: HEALTH

1. 'Women with dementia receive less medical attention', ucl.ac.uk.
2. 'Association of surgeon-patient sex concordance with postoperative outcomes', jamanetwork.com.
3. 'New taskforce to level-up maternity care and tackle disparities', www.gov.uk.
4. 'Depressive disorder (depression)', who.int.
5. 'The female happiness paradox', nber.org.
6. 'Up to one million women in Great Britain at risk of gambling harms', begambleware.org.

CHAPTER 10: WORK

1. 'Gender pay gap in the UK: 2022: differences in pay between women and men by age, region, full-time and part-time, and occupation', ons.gov.uk.
2. 'Barely any change to gender earnings gap in last 25 years once you account for increases in women's education', ifs.og.uk.
3. 'Gender pay gap in U.S. hasn't changed much in two decades', pewresearch.org.
4. 'Pay transparency can address the gender pay gap', ilo.org.
5. 'Childbearing for women born in different years, England and Wales: 2020', ons.gov.uk.
   The Female Lead collaborated with Dr Madeleine Wyatt and King's College Business School for the hybrid working study.

CHAPTER 11: MONEY

1. 'Barely any change to gender earnings gap in last 25 years once you account for increases in women's education', ifs.og.uk.
2. 'Raising UK state pension age to 66 has seen big increase in working 65-year-olds, but particularly deprived women', theconversation.com.
3. 'Secret billionaires: the executive power gap revealed', thefemalelead.com.

CHAPTER 12: SOCIETY

1. 'Global, regional, and national prevalence estimates of physical or sexual, or both, intimate partner violence against women in 2018', thelancet.com.

CHAPTER 13: THE BIG PICTURE

1. 'Women CEOs of the S&P 500 (list)', catalyst.org.
2. 'Fewer than a third of UN member states have ever had a woman leader', pewresearch.org.
3. 'Equality, diversity and student characteristics data: students at English higher education providers between 2010-11 and 2020-21', office for students.org.uk.
4. 'Progress on the Sustainable Development Goals: the gender snapshot 2022', unwomen.org.
5. 'Women CEOs: leadership for a diverse future', spglobal.com.
6. 'The female economy', hbr.org.
7. 'Components of GDP: key economic indicators', commonslibraryparliament.uk.
8. 'United States private consumption: % of GDP', ceicdata.com.
9. 'When women lead, firms win', spglobal.com.

CHAPTER 14: ECONOMIC POWER

1. 'Fawcett's 2022 sex and power index reveals that less than 1/3 of UK's top jobs are filled by women', fawcettsociety.org.uk.
2. 'More women than ever launched companies in 2022, Rose Review reveals', natwestgroup.com.
3. 'Male-owned businesses get seven times more funding that those owned by women', startups.co.uk.
4. 'Alarming lack of women in executive roles despite FTSE 350 improving boardroom gender diversity', cranfield.ac.uk.
5. Secret billionaires: the executive power gap revealed', thefemalelead.com.
6. 'The top richest women in the world 2022', forbes.com.
7. 'Shattering the glass screen', mckinsey.com.
8. 'The women in social media exec boards', postbeyond.com.
9. 'Women over 50; the right to be seen on screen', seejane.org.

10. 'Social media audiences in the United Kingdom as of January 2023, by gender', statista.com.
11. 'Average daily time spent by users worldwide on social media apps from October 2023 to March 2023, by gender', statista.com.

CHAPTER 15: DECISION-MAKING POWER

1. 'Fewer than a third of UN member states have ever had a woman leader', pewresearch.org.
2. 'Women in politics and public life', commonslibrary.parliament.uk.
3. 'Gender balance in politics', instituteforgovernment.org.uk.
4. 'Facts and figures: women's leadership and political participation', unwomen.org.
5. 'House of Commons trends: the age of MPs', commonslibrary.parliament.uk.

CHAPTER 16: WHAT THIS WORLD COULD LOOK LIKE

1. K. A. Bratton and L. P. Ray, 2002. 'Descriptive representation: policy outcomes and municipal day-care coverage in Norway', *American Journal of Political Science*, 46(2), 428–437.
2. 'What women want: tackling gender equalities in unpaid care and the workplace', progressive-policy.net.
3. 'Percentage of the population in England who gave to charity from 2013/14 to 2021/22, by gender', statista.com.
4. 'Research: women are better leaders during a crisis', hbr.org.
5. 'Women CEOs: leadership for a diverse future', spglobal.com.